To Tony Kostreba

THE THIRD TESTAMENT
A METAPARADIGM

My brother Tony, totally appreciate the support. Thank you. May you continue being just as you are, many may not understand you, but you're an amazing guy.

GURMAN

May you enjoy reading this book as I enjoyed writing it. Love You

08/04/20

BALBOA.PRESS
A DIVISION OF HAY HOUSE

Copyright © 2020 Gurman.

All rights reserved. No part of this book may be used or reproduced by any means, graphic, electronic, or mechanical, including photocopying, recording, taping or by any information storage retrieval system without the written permission of the author except in the case of brief quotations embodied in critical articles and reviews.

Scripture taken from the King James Version of the Bible

Balboa Press books may be ordered through booksellers or by contacting:

Balboa Press
A Division of Hay House
1663 Liberty Drive
Bloomington, IN 47403
www.balboapress.com
1 (877) 407-4847

Because of the dynamic nature of the Internet, any web addresses or links contained in this book may have changed since publication and may no longer be valid. The views expressed in this work are solely those of the author and do not necessarily reflect the views of the publisher, and the publisher hereby disclaims any responsibility for them.

The author of this book does not dispense medical advice or prescribe the use of any technique as a form of treatment for physical, emotional, or medical problems without the advice of a physician, either directly or indirectly. The intent of the author is only to offer information of a general nature to help you in your quest for emotional and spiritual well-being. In the event you use any of the information in this book for yourself, which is your constitutional right, the author and the publisher assume no responsibility for your actions.

Any people depicted in stock imagery provided by Getty Images are models, and such images are being used for illustrative purposes only. Certain stock imagery © Getty Images.

Print information available on the last page.

ISBN: 978-1-9822-3569-7 (sc)
ISBN: 978-1-9822-3568-0 (hc)
ISBN: 978-1-9822-3570-3 (e)

Library of Congress Control Number: 2020909086

Balboa Press rev. date: 05/27/2020

To my daughter Tiyi. Sometimes I wonder if I am here for you or if you came for me. Continue to be guided by the compass inside and not the dictates of what's gone but what's to come. Walk your path with authority.

CONTENTS

Foreword ix
Preface xiii
Acknowledgments xvii
Introduction xix

Chapter 1   Understanding Concepts 1
Chapter 2   Significance of Context 17
Chapter 3   The Power of Words 27
Chapter 4   The Concept of God 33
Chapter 5   What/Who Actually Is This God? 59
Chapter 6   The Historical Jesus versus the Theological
             Concept 91
Chapter 7   A Brief Historical Perspective 113
Chapter 8   The Birth of Heresy 123
Chapter 9   The Christ Concept 129
Chapter 10   The Concept of Death 143
Chapter 11   Life after Death 153
Chapter 12   Heaven and Hell 165

Conclusion 173
References 177

FOREWORD

I have been involved in spiritual experiences in one way or another for as long as I can remember, but I have been involved in formal church ministry since 1982, when I made the critical decision to surrender my life to God.

In 1991, I became a licensed minister, and in 1993, I was ordained as the first woman in the 103-year history of a local Baptist church in a small town in Pennsylvania. Consequently, I went to seminary, where I studied rigorously until I got my doctor of ministry degree.

I spent years in classrooms with professors who challenged and stretched me in a way that can be described only as mental and emotional torture. What made matters worse was that I felt there was very little spiritual substance to balance out these intense theological calisthenics. I cosigned onto the experience because I thought it was necessary to do things the right way and be accepted as a woman in ministry at a time when it wasn't popular. I was wrong.

During that time, I consistently challenged the status quo mainly because I was having supernatural and spiritual experiences that could not be explained or denied. I refrained from being a part of the good ole boys' network but for more than the obvious reasons. I felt I didn't belong there, and I didn't subscribe to the philosophies or methodologies being done in the name of the gospel that left many crushed and consumed.

Then I realized why this system did not work for me; it was because I was not a part of it. I had a very different motivation for doing my work; I simply wanted to love and serve others. That was it! I made incredible sacrifices for this cause. I emptied myself. I poured out my gifts, talents, and abilities on those who on rare occasions showed gratitude. But I wouldn't change a thing.

All my formal theological training and experience has boiled down to one thing—you're not living until you are giving. Serving others is my religion, and it gives me a great sense of purpose. I have enormous gratitude for the opportunity to love and accept others, especially when they needed it the most, and I strive every day to be better at it.

Although it is spiritually, emotionally, and mentally gratifying, God and nature reward me physiologically with the release of oxytocin (nature's feel-good hormone that adds meaning to my life and reduces stress). Could it be possible that I'm addicted to it?

After twenty-three years of pastoral ministry, I find myself in a unique place. I did everything I thought was right as a professional in ministry, but I did not get the outcomes I had hoped for, all for good reasons. I learned that the man-made system of the modern-day church for the most part was broken and in need of reconstitution and not just because it mimicked much of what looks like a capitalistic machine. But I believe this is because the church has lost its focus and reason for existence and in its current state will continue to be irrelevant to and ineffective for the masses.

I have learned through my research, study, and experience that we need something greater than ourselves to achieve, but there are no absolutes regarding how that plays out for each individual. I have been in an intimate relationship with God most of my life, but I pray that I never let that spiritual connection become bigger than the respectful, humane treatment of others who share the planet. Yet we can all attest to the fact that many an atrocity has been committed because of what was thought to be the one and only way without regard for the sanctity of human life. This should be troubling.

The intriguing material that Bernard Marshall presents as Gurman in *The Third Testament* is a plethora of spiritual concepts that forces us to look at what is deemed right through a personal refining process. He presents revelatory information that challenges our current belief systems to help us get to the place of pure and utter resolve. His approach commands us to whittle our way down to the lowest common denominator and helps us understand that there is only one true religion, the religion of love. Until we practice that, it doesn't matter what we label ourselves—we are spiritually inauthentic.

If I had to use one word to describe Gurman, it would be *free*. He has taken the courage to challenge the status quo and think outside the box as a liberated thinker. His powerful voice needs no stamp of approval from anyone. He is a prophet in his own right.

Gurman's in-depth contributions to the discussion of truths are well grounded as he offers a panoramic view of what exists and lead us to the possibility of what will be. He leaves no stone unturned as his genius reminds us that modern science has already torn to shreds many of our long-held beliefs in the same way Christopher Columbus did in the Middle Ages when he annihilated the archaic belief that the earth was flat.

I applaud Gurman for his efforts to wrestle with long-standing beliefs with such depth and breadth that challenges us and makes us determine what we believe and why. He invites us to evaluate and investigate what we believe and think to be true; but he doesn't just leave us there; he gives us a wealth of raw material with which to do our work. His brilliance is pronounced on every page as he expounds with ease on topics that some consider foreign ideals and forces us to continue to turn each page with utter curiosity.

Make no mistake; Gurman need not be compared to anyone. He is in a class by himself and should be considered one of the leading voices and one to watch now and well into the twenty-second century if but for only one reason—he dared offer another testament of the possibility of truth, and for this, he is to be commended. And in the end, we will find that his absolute motivation can be summed up in love.

Dr. LaVerne Adams
DMin, CEO and Master Certification Life Coach
Total Life Consultancy LLC
www.TotalLifeConsultancy.com

PREFACE

It is amazing how time and space sometimes appear irrelevant when we consider life-changing events. Throughout life, we face many situations and circumstances; some we may appreciate and call good while others we call not so good.

It's normal to recollect life events that evoked emotional reactions. These memories subsequently leave an indelible stain on our minds. But how do we explain the life events that may not have been traumatic, distressing, or deeply emotional but were so overwhelmingly profound that they may have altered our lives forever?

I have had quite a few experiences I could so categorize, but one experience played a significant role in directing my life's journey along a distinct path. It was responsible for planting the seed for this book and my endeavors along this path. I can describe such a path only as miraculous and mystical.

I recall as a boy sharing a bedroom with my elder brother. One night at around 7:30, I discovered a red, hard-covered Bible in the room. I asked other members of the household whose it was, but no one claimed it. That was understandable since no one in the house was religiously inclined. I was overjoyed. I decided I would make this Bible my personal Bible and read and study portions of it every night until I read it all and knew everything there was to know about God. Nothing too fascinating about that, but what was amazing was the thoughts that followed.

Our neighbors were the Ramnanans, devout Hindus. Every morning, I observed Mr. Ramnanan perform his religious ritual. To the front of his home was a well-constructed shrine with statues of what in his religion were termed deities. As night follows day, Mr. Ramnanan would pick fresh flowers from his garden to commune with his gods in his customary manner.

That was incredible to me; no one in my household ever displayed such discipline as it pertains to prayer, devotion, or anything religious for that matter. The closest I had ever come to anything spiritual in my home was my mother's periodic smoking-out of our home that I later learned was called smudging. It was something I don't think even she understood.

Another phenomenon was the odd scent that we would get in the house every so often, especially after a funeral in the cemetery, which was just around the corner from where we lived. When that occurred, I would hear my mother cussing and telling whomever was apparently visiting to leave. Sometimes, I would get a bit scared by that, but I never dared to show it.

I had some other very unusual experiences I will mention in this book, but I did not have a disciplined spiritual program such as Mr. Ramnanan's.

To the east of our house was Mr. Asgarali, the principal of a Muslim primary school and a hajji. *Hajji* is an honorific given to a Muslim who has successfully completed a hajj to Mecca, one of the pillars of Islam. It is traditionally used to refer to an elder because it can take time for Muslims to accumulate the money required for such travel, especially in that era when the notion of simply traveling on a plane was a colossal event. In a fashion similar to that of Mr. Ramnanan, Mr. Asgarali was devout, dedicated, and above all disciplined in his spiritual inclination. On Fridays, whether rain or shine, he could be seen journeying to the mosque for Friday prayer or *Jummah*.

The most outstanding factor to me however was how his religious persuasion seemed to extend to all areas of his life. Mr. Asgarali was always well mannered, and his entire being reflected serenity and peace. He was always impeccably clean; his garb was always lily-white, matching his hair and beard.

The depth of my religious knowledge was the result of the Presbyterian primary school I attended and the odd Sundays when I would attend Roman Catholic or Anglican churches. Notwithstanding, my insights into deeper spiritual matters were initiated by my association with Mr. Nato, who is deceased. He was known as a man of high science who was more than met the eye. The things I saw Mr. Nato do spanned way outside the dimensions of Newtonian science. Just being around him was a magical experience I never totally understood at age eleven, but it afforded me credible insight into a realm beyond what we can see and touch. Subsequently, herein lies the framework for my future path and soul's purpose. After all, despite how it may appear, all things occur according to divine order.

My thoughts raced in my head regarding these men on that momentous night in my bedroom when I was deeply inspired to know who this God was. I wondered, *How can there be only one God when everyone seems completely convinced that his or her way of serving the divine is the right way?* All practices appeared so distinct from one another. I heard in my mind, *This is your task. Fix it.*

Based on my severely limited outlook, knowledge, and experience in anything of any true significance, I decided to read the entire Bible and note where I believed the disparity began. In my limited scope and understanding I thought that everything started from the Bible and that somewhere along the line, people had misconstrued what was written, which led to the variations and diversity of religious persuasions we see today.

That night, a seed was planted in me that took root and influenced my life's journey on which I became a seeker of all matters concerning who or what God is, a journey that meant the understanding of the self and that what we were was no different from what God is. This journey started without but culminated within. It became a journey from the head to the heart during which I saw close friends and family fall away. But these instances were not influential enough to steer me from the path. This book is but a portion of that journey based on a seed planted over thirty-three years ago.

ACKNOWLEDGMENTS

There are many to acknowledge when it comes to this book since the seed for it was planted over thirty years ago, but some continued to remind me in diverse ways, sometimes consciously and sometimes not, of the necessity to have started it, and they provided the impetuous I needed to complete it.

Sheldon Blake, I don't think any other person has believed in me as much as and for as long as you have. You believed in me before I existed. Opal Jasper, your continued encouragement at the most significant times would never go unacknowledged. Ms. Kemi Thomas, if only I could see what you see in me; words would be unable to describe my stature. You entered my life when I was at my lowest and continued to be a bastion of support throughout. Thank you for being there to provide the reassurance I needed. You're the epitome of what it means to be a friend, God knows that you are much more than that to me.

Dr. Cindy Trimm, my mother, mentor, and guide, the first person to look me in my eyes and say, "I believe in you," you told me on more than one occasion that I needed to write, that I had books in me that needed expression. Gratitude to my baba, mentor, and disciplinarian Mr. Michael Maxima; indeed, the consciousness of the universe is beyond our comprehension. You have been my citadel and admonisher where this book was concerned and beyond.

Ms. Gelita Mimms, many times, we don't recognize how going about our business diligently can be the best guidance we can give another. Your drive and passion for your own vision in film served as the impetus for me to pursue this agenda to completion. You were always encouraging; you read excerpts and said that it was compelling and that I needed to keep going.

Sheldon Mendoza, thanks for always speaking your truth. Many times, your utterances helped me recognize that I wasn't going crazy. Cornelius Williams aka 'Corn,' if I was Moses you would be Aaron, thank you for your patience, support, contributions and yeoman service, you kept my hands up when I grew weary. Finally to Mrs. D'Juana Dudley, although your input in my life was in the latter stages, its significance cannot be compared. The interest you have shown in me, my work, and what I consider to be my God-given mandate will never go unnoticed.

Thank you all.

INTRODUCTION

Before I began writing this book, I observed in myself subtle feelings of apprehension, tension, and unease. Initially, I did not recognize why I was feeling that way. My experience would have taught me however to explore the cause of these emotions in a bid to understand why. On self-examination, I realized that their existed some deep-seated underlying fears in me—a fear of the thoughts of society toward what was written; a fear of not being understood, ostracized, and labeled; and a fear of having my character assassinated and not accepted.

In the midst of this pondering and internal wrangling, I heard quite distinctly the following words in my mind: *I am the only authority*, and for weeks, that statement reverberated in my heart and mind. I contemplated those words and wondered about their significance and meaning. What was I hearing intuitively? Before long, it all started to make sense. Even though all that is contained herein is based on guidance and inspiration I received from divine intelligence, what was written would also be greatly opposed. Not that its contents are flawed or fictitious in any way, but its revelations may be unable to fit in the present paradigm of many.

The revelations in my spirit of *I am the only authority* meant that even though many might disagree with what is contained herein, one's disagreement is not an indicator of one's authority and does not invalidate the contents of this book.

Many of us have unconsciously taken over the position of God (which also happens to be a concept given to us and one we would explore further) even though we would never admit it. We tell ourselves that what we know is all there is to know, and as such, any knowledge or information that cannot be assimilated into our present schema is flawed and inaccurate, making the information ungodly and the messenger heathenish. Such thinking is simply a result of ignorance and a product of fear, a fear that at most times goes even beyond the subconscious and is brought about by generations of conditioning.

In the scientific world, a theoretical postulation is the best given explanation for a specified phenomenon, bearing in mind that theories are not absolutes and though they may have existed for quite some time are subject to change. Theories are only as accurate as the testable variables or identified causes presented. A theoretical hypothesis may indicate that poverty is the primary cause of criminal behavior, for instance, whilst other variables such as a lack of education and one's culturing might also be considered. However, coming to such a conclusion is restricted to the identified variables.

There may have been numerous other variables that researchers failed to consider or identify as possible causes for a phenomenon. As a result, considerable subjectivity serves as a critical factor in structuring a research method, a process that is ultimately designed to yield objective results. With this in mind, one can only wonder if there can ever be any true objectivity. Such is the case not only with the scientific world but with the religious world as well.

Our world is in a state of perpetual decadence, and though many may say that such is a sign of the times, historical research shows that such has been our global state for quite some time. If we are to take the biblical narrative of Adam and Eve as outlined in Genesis as fact, it would mean that a murder occurred when there was only four persons on the planet; that translates to a murder rate ratio of 1:4. Further, this murder involved siblings, making it a total collapse of the family structure. Notwithstanding, we were told of a war in the heavens, a coup d'état of sorts prior to our earthly existence; that in itself begs us to wonder if conflict and war are inevitable realities since even in heaven there was war.

Various historical accounts can be identified to show humankind's destruction, annihilation, mayhem, and onslaught against each other, nature, the ecosystem, and ourselves. From the savagery of the Paleolithic and Mesolithic hunter-gatherer communities to the barbarianism of the Neolithic and Bronze Age farmers, the saga continued. From the Crusades and the Inquisitions to the Jewish Holocaust, Hiroshima and Nagasaki, the Mongol invasions of Asia and Europe, World Wars I and II, chattel slavery, and violence that perpetuated the civil rights movement and more contemporarily the Jihadists and ISIS. This list outlines major historical conflicts, but let's not forget our daily wars of neighbor versus neighbor, husbands versus wives, and sibling rivalry. Further, there is violence against ourselves via alcoholism, drug use, gluttony, and sexual and emotional abuse, bearing in mind that our destruction still does not conclude there.

This is simply the gross manifestation of our destruction, of acts of extreme cruelty perpetuated on one by another and on ourselves however our destruction exists on various levels. When one observes the desecration of the ecosystem; annihilation of plant and wildlife; pollution of the land, skies, and seas; and deforestation and the like, it is clear that we are destined on a clear collision course.

In a leaked encyclical of June 2015, even Pope Francis declared,

> The Earth is protesting for the wrong that we are doing to her, because of the irresponsible use and abuse of the goods that God has placed on her. We have grown up thinking that we were her owners and dominators, authorized to loot her. The violence that exists in the human heart, wounded by sin, is also manifest in the symptoms of illness that we see in the Earth, the water, the air and in living things.[1]

Some might ask on what moral authority the pope and the entire Catholic body could make such pronouncements. Historically, the Catholic Church has been identified as a major contributor to the destruction and demise of many nations and peoples. Notwithstanding, that body continues to conceal vital historical data and information that could be critical in perpetuating a major paradigm shift of contemporary society's collective consciousness.

It is written in Ephesians 6:12 (KJV), "For we wrestle not against flesh and blood, but against principalities, against powers, against the rulers of the darkness of this world, against spiritual wickedness in high places." If this scripture is true, how is it relevant or applicable to our societal dilemma? The state of our society is simply a reflection of the state of our selves; humans are conduits, channels for something unseen, and the state of humankind's consciousness that acts as a filter or as the lens through which all

---

[1] Yardley, Jim and Elisabetta, Povoledo. "Leak of Pope's Encyclical on climate change hints at tension in Vatican." New York Times, June 16, 2015. https://www.nytimes.com/2015/06/17/world/europe/leak-of-pope-francis-encyclical-hints-at-tensions-in-vatican.html.

things are perceived determines the state of our society and what we know as reality. As a result, humans biggest enemies are ourselves, and our most detrimental liability is our ignorance.

Hosea 4:6 (KJV) states, "My people perish for a lack of knowledge." Chinese military general strategist Sun Tzu declared, "If ignorant both of your enemy and yourself, you are certain to be in peril."[2] Johann Wolfgang Von Goeffe stated, "There is nothing more frightful than ignorance in action."[3] According to the Dalai Lama, "Where ignorance is our master, there can be no possibility of real peace."[4] In the words of Confucius, "Ignorance is the night of the mind, but a night without moon or star."[5] Many may argue that knowledge got us here in the first place and that ignorance is bliss since our increase in knowledge has allowed us to undertake some very destructive agendas.

Knowledge in science allowed us to understand the inner workings of the atom and led to the eventual development of the atomic bomb and its subsequent use in Hiroshima and Nagasaki. Knowledge of DNA and the genetic code led to genetic manipulation and our false confidence of being like the gods endowed with the ability to manipulate humankind's original design. With this knowledge, we lied to ourselves and to the general population, insisting that now we were capable of making people better and healthier when it was by our own hands that people became diseased in the first instance.

---

[2] Tzu, Sun. "The Art of War." Canterbury Classics. May 1, 2014.

[3] Goethe, Johan W. "Selected Poems, Goethe, The Collected Works Vol. 1." Princeton University Press. 1994.

[4] Singh, M. P. "Quote Unquote_Handbook of Famous Quotations." Lotus Press. 2006.

[5] Dawson, Menender M. "The Ethics of Confucius." Forgotten Books, February 27, 2010.

Because of knowledge, we were able to design and manufacture high-powered rifles and other handguns with the sole intention to kill and subsequently convince ourselves that such was designed to save lives. Despite the outlined disadvantages, advancements in knowledge and science are not without advantages.

Generally speaking, however, it is clear that knowledge without context and direction can serve as a detriment rather than a benefit. It is for this reason that two of Gandhi's seven cardinal sins included knowledge without character and science without morality since both knowledge and science minus a conscious compass can be counterproductive and destructive and can have more disastrous consequences than ignorance. It is one thing for a person to not know, but it is something worse for a person to not know and not know he or she doesn't know. This book is an attempt to eradicate the prevailing ignorance, to shed light on the wanton darkness that prevents the human from truly being, and to align knowledge on a divine path that leads to greater harmony, societal cohesion, congruence, and peace toward wholeness or holiness.

The depth and complexity of our present quagmire needs to be unraveled meticulously and delicately since evil has become fair seeming. Such concurs with Surah 15. Al-Hijr, Ayah of the Quran, states, "[Iblis] said, 'O my Lord! Because Thou hast put me in the wrong I will make [wrong] fair-seeming to them on the earth and I will put them all in the wrong.'" Every aspect of our world has been turned upside down and we are none the wiser. When such occurs, presenting what is true and correct is usually met with great resistance and adversity since our conditioning has occurred generationally and has gone beyond simply the cognitive. The extent of our conditioning encompasses the cellular level and has gone to the depths of the soulular blemishing our very souls and psyche.

Humanity has become nothing more than sheeple; the major portion of our brains has become insignificant and redundant while the little percentage we utilize is entrapped in retention, regurgitation, and other paltry trappings. We were subsequently classified into categories based on illusionary concepts such as class, race, and status. Rather than identifying with the light that shines within to establish our true identity, everything external to us has now become the milestone for our uniqueness. John 1:5 epitomizes this condition: "And the light shineth in the darkness; and the darkness comprehended it not." As such, a hierarchical structure was established that initially began as law segregating human beings into categories of social class, which eventually became the upper, middle, and lower classes designed to unconsciously establish one's worth and identity while simultaneously maintaining the ideology of divide and rule.

According to philosopher Karl Marx, class is determined entirely by one's relationship to the means of production with the proletarians being those who work but do not own the means of production and the bourgeoisie being those who invest and live off the surplus generated by the former. This hierarchical structure or identity construct would be further subdivided in various ways but would also give rise to various deep-seated psychological, emotional, and spiritual consequences throughout the generations.

As a result of this flawed sociological construct, humanity erroneously redefined what it meant to be wealthy and successful in relation to possessions and positions. People were now driven to establish an ego identity based on materialism and other external factors with no regard for their fellowmen or the consequences that follow many of their actions. A flawed concept of what it means to be successful, educated, healthy, and spiritual has become judicial notice the essence of which is not even questioned. All structures that make up societal systems have been undermined making them unreliable and illogical. Weak, unsound, and erroneous taglines were developed and accepted as our guiding principles such as the end justifies the means and get rich or die trying all with the objective of being identified with a particular class while distancing and separating ourselves from the collective whole. Whether consciously or unconsciously, people now strive to attain this mirage of an identity to become somebodies, and that implies unconsciously that they are nobodies.

Man-made appointments, titles, and letters to one's name have become the index by which prestige and authority are bestowed, and as a result, such demarcations divide the intelligent from the unintelligent. Only the distinct few, the crème de la crème, products of the Ivy Leagues can truly make intelligent pronouncements where they themselves are being hoodwinked by the mirage of being persons of significance and authority in the context of being better than those who do not belong to that category.

To further enshrine this intellectual divide, particular vernacular and jargon were developed for scholarly disciplines and replaced common terminologies of understanding automatically ostracizing the greater percentage of the population while maintaining and further establishing ignorance of a system that at best can be described as nothing short of evil.

The whole design appears to be well planned and thought out for eons by what I would call at this stage an unseen hand. Our global population has been blinded and misdirected as we focus on the irrelevant and mundane, and by our own accord, we unconsciously maintain and sustain that system that leads to our demise, clearly the Hegelian dialectic principle[6] at work. Indeed, a battle is taking place, but this battle is not about race, class, possession, or position; this war is not about developed or developing states; this is not a war of religions, of crusades and jihads. This battle is deeper and beyond what the eyes can see. This is a battle and an all-out war for control of our very souls.

---

[6] Developed by Georg Wilhelm Friedrich Hegel. The Hegelian dialectic is the framework for guiding our thoughts and actions into conflicts that lead us to a predetermined solution.

CHAPTER 1
UNDERSTANDING CONCEPTS

I have never let my schooling interfere with my education.

—Mark Twain

The Foundation of Our Knowledge

As with the construction of any sturdy and valuable building, the first and most integral factor is its foundation. A building can have the most elaborate walls, roof, windows and doors, tile, molding, and other fixtures, but if its foundation is unstable, it will be unable to stand solidly. This is especially so if the building is complex and intricate.

If the structure in question is a simple tent, a foundation of sand might be sufficient. However, as the objectives evolve—and evolve they must since all things evolve whether we accept that or not—the simplicity of that tent established on sand would be insufficient to meet the expanded needs for which it was originally designed. It would be foolhardy, however, to develop the tent into a more ostentatious structure without first considering its foundation.

As unfortunate as it may seem, this is exactly what we have done and continue to do in our personal lives and by extension in our society. Our personal evolution automatically perpetuates greater insights and advancements in science, technology, and spirituality, but we remain rooted in a static foundation that cannot withstand the dynamism of this continuous evolution. As we grow consciously however, we learn and understand more recognizing that the things we once accepted as absolute and took as judicial notice were not necessarily so, yet many of these outdated and flawed ideologies continue to shape our perceptions and guide our worldviews.

Before focusing on our external world, we must understand our internal world. This internal world exists in various levels or degrees bearing in mind that the state of the seen is always a result of the state of the unseen. In the words of Marcus Garvey,[7] "It is only through the root can one determine the quality of the fruit." The unseen root, which lies below the earth's surface, is one of the many unseen aspects of the tree that is critical to the state of the tree and the quality of the fruit. The same can be said of a building. The depth and strength of the foundation identify its durability and state. Rene Descartes, in his *Meditations on First Philosophy*, stated, "Once the foundations of a building are undermined, anything built on them collapses of its own accord."[8]

One of the primary mechanisms that is critical to our foundation is our minds. In the words of Napoleon Hill,[9] "Mind is the one thing that separates the human being from any animal." Being blind or not having any limbs in no way determines our humanness, but the fact that we are thinking creatures, that we are conscious

---

[7] Marcus Mosiah Garvey Jr., ONH, was a Jamaican-born political activist, publisher, journalist, entrepreneur, and orator.

[8] Descartes, René. "Meditations of First Philosophy with selections from the objections and replies." Cambridge University Press, 1996.

[9] Oliver Napoleon Hill (1883–1970) was an American self-help author. He is known best for his book *Think and Grow Rich*.

of our consciousness, does. The degree of our awareness and our consciousness, however, determines our state of humanness. We have the capacity of being high among the gods or of being low among the fallen. Such a state is a choice we all have, and it is determined by our degree of consciousness.

With this understanding, it is easy to comprehend why there seems to have been a concerted effort to ensure that most people in society are non-thinkers and that our ability to use our minds appears restricted to regurgitation and recollection thereby keeping the collective consciousness below the threshold of our natural capacity. No longer are we thinking beings but robotic recorders. No longer do we have a voice; we have now become simply echoes. What we don't recognize is the state that we are in is a result of the choices we made and continue to make, which maintains our state of helplessness and hopelessness.

Our Mental State

Our awareness determines our thoughts, which establish our beliefs, and shape our attitudes, which determine our behavior. What are the variables, however, from which our thoughts are derived? Both nature and nurture are critical determinants in this equation. And when we expand beyond the psychological and the sociological to include the spiritual, further insights would be attained that would aid in a more holistic understanding.

Without exploring further in this sphere just yet, there are some basic factors we need to understand. According to Anaïs Nin,[10] "We

---

[10] Anaïs Nin was a French–Cuban American diarist, essayist, novelist, and writer of short stories and erotica.

don't see things as they are, we see them as we are." It means that all sensory stimuli derived from our external environment whether tangible or experiential are defined, interpreted, or perceived according to the degree of our consciousness and do not necessarily reflect the absolute truth about what is observed or experienced.

The mechanical process whereby stimuli excite sensory neurons and send electrical messages to our brains is significant but meaningless. By meaningless, I mean that its meaning is defined subjectively due to our conditioning. As a result, our mental state acts as the lens through which we see and which formulates our conclusion—a conclusion that can be very real and may also appear to be true. Our reality then, which is determined perceptually, is not necessarily the truth; it may or may not, however, serve to our advantage.

Precepts and concepts within context shape reality. This is our foundation, and if our foundations are flawed, so will our conclusions be. The story is told of twin boys whose father was an alcoholic. The boys were the same genetically and shared similar experiences since they were both weaned and cultured in the same environment. As adults, however, one became an alcoholic similar to his father while the other totally abstained from alcohol. The question then asked was, "How come these two boys, who by nature shared the same genetic structure and who by nurture were cultured in similar fashion, took such divergent paths?"

Our ignorance, experiences, conditioning, culturing, hurts, and pains sometimes establish certain references that allow for biases that determine our states. Nothing in life has any meaning other than the meaning we give it. What are the factors then that are responsible for determining the meaning we give to our experiences? Why in death do some mourn while others rejoice? Why do poverty and lack in childhood perpetuate greater lack in some making them victims of circumstances to the point of hating the world and subsequently leading lives of crime or negativity while others weaned in similar circumstances refuse to be defined by such and strive for greatness?

The answer to these apparent contradictions is simple. As in the case of the twin boys whose father was an alcoholic, they shared similar experiences but their perspectives on those experiences were different. The way either boy defined the same situation yielded diverse viewpoints, which subsequently directed the courses of their lives in opposite directions.

The way we perceive and define things is highly contingent on our precepts and concepts. These intangibilities lay the foundation on which we all stand, shape our worldviews, and unconsciously lead our thoughts, establish our beliefs, form our values and attitudes, and ultimately guide and direct our behaviors. These abstract terminologies direct and influence whatever comes to us in terms of information and content the relevance of which is dependent on the framework or context in which it is obtained. Our concepts and precepts are our terms of reference. This is our foundation, and if our foundations were flawed as was previously outlined, so would our conclusion be despite how educated or informed we might be.

Abstract Terminologies

As a result, it is only until we can gain a comprehensive understanding of these abstract terminologies and how they shape the way that we think—or prevent us from thinking—that we would be able to see things in a more holistic manner. Doing so allows us to change the lens through which we see, question what we have been and continue to be taught, and redefine what we have been conditioned to accept for generations. Until that is done, expanding our knowledge in any sphere would ultimately be redundant since the lens through which all such information is directed would be tainted by our foundational concepts.

Ever wonder why someone who is very qualified according to the ideology outlined by our current educational system is not very intelligent? Many of us may have never even considered the difference between being educated, certified, qualified, and intelligent. Until we stop for a minute to consider the precepts and concepts we accept in any context, all that we perceive is flawed. All our noble attempts to find solutions for discord, conflict, and societal ills would continue to perpetuate greater problems while the erroneous line espoused by our policy makers in response to such would continue to be that this is the price of progress.

From the perspectives of most if not all religious and scientific doctrines, the human being has been identified as the most intelligent of creation. Maybe the notion of being the most intelligent is inherent in his design. Maybe this is his innate potential. However, his current state clearly does not depict or reflect such stature. Until this divine conduit identified as man—and by that I mean humanity—recognizes and acknowledges his divinity and comes to a greater understanding of his self, his makeup, and his design taking all facets of his being into consideration and subsequently making an effort to evolve consciously in all spheres of existence, all thoughts and actions would be emanating from a place of deficiency and low frequency.

There was never a time in history when humanity existed in its highest vibrational state expressing the fullness of their potential or divinity. As outlined by Helen Keller,[11] though we may have eyes, we were never really able to see. Let us now bit by bit and layer by layer deconstruct our present foundation and attempt to redesign a more refined and holistic foundation that no longer restricts or limits the divinity of humanity. Starting with the foundation of our understanding, we look at what exactly are precepts and concepts and subsequently analyze some of the abstract variables that have guided our lives and that we have accepted for generations without question although we lacked understanding of their meaning.

What Are Precepts?

> Precept: Late 14c., from Old French *percept, percet* (12c.), from Latin *praeceptum* "maxim, rule of conduct, order," noun use of neuter past participle of *praecipere* "give rules to, order, advise," literally "take beforehand," from *prae* "before" (see *pre-*) + *capere* (past participle *captus*) "to take," from PIE root *kap-* "to grasp."

A precept is a commandment or direction given as a rule of action; it is an injunction as to moral conduct or a maxim. As outlined in its definition, it is taken beforehand; it precedes anything that

---

[11] Helen Adams Keller (1880–1968) was an American author, political activist, and lecturer. She was the first deaf-blind person to earn a Bachelor of Arts degree.

subsequently comes to us in whatever manner and subsequently shapes such.

As rules of action, precepts direct our behavior, which implies that they govern our thoughts since thought must precede action though some of our actions sometimes question the very existence of thought.

Precepts are the determining factor for one's form; they lay a foundation that guides our worldview. Precepts are critical determinants in everything we do since they basically guide all decisions we make.

Precepts Outlined

Precepts are rules that determine how people should behave. They are general rules intended to regulate behavior or thought. They are rules or principles for action. They are guides or rules for morals.

Our precepts are critical factors that form abstract objects and regulate our thoughts that control our actions. They are the foundation of our knowledge, and since they control our thoughts, they determine what we believe and what we don't believe. Our precepts are fundamental to our knowledge and beliefs, and as such, we should be aware of the meaning and basis of the precepts we accept. The precepts that govern our lives are given to us and accepted without question. They may have originated from an accepted authority be it philosophical, scientific, or religious. This process occurs in an almost automatic and unconscious manner that shapes the psyche of the collective consciousness of society.

Numerous precepts can be identified in various religious bodies, and some of these precepts can be considered binding on their followers. Failing to adhere to these principles according to the faith may lead to ostracism or even death. Of the over forty thousand Christian denominations, there exist various precepts between them including the precept of the Ten Commandments. The Roman Catholic Church outlines five basic precepts:

- Attending Mass on Sundays and on holy days of obligation
- Confessing sins at least once a year
- Receiving the sacrament of the Eucharist at least once during the Easter season
- Observing the days of fasting and abstinence established by the church
- Providing for the needs of the church

In Islam, there are also various precepts governed by five major ones.

- Shahada: faith
- Salah: prayer
- Zakat: charity
- Sawm: fasting
- Hajj: pilgrimage

And so too is Buddhism:

- Harming living things
- Taking what is not given
- Sexual misconduct
- Lying or gossiping
- Taking intoxicating substances such as drugs or drink

As positive and well assuming as precepts appear to be, they can have a totally diverse or contrary effect that can be used to divide and perpetuate conflict. Following precepts according to the letter can lead to various moral dilemmas, especially in our evolving society. Take Christianity for instance. The man/male is identified as the head of the home, more than likely, this principle would have been established by a man, but what if the man had some accident or debilitating illness rendering him mentally unsound? Would he still be identified as the head of the home? I have always had the issue with the commandment thou shalt not kill, but if I don't kill, how am I to eat? What about the Buddhist precept of not lying? Suppose lying might save the life of another such as a victim of domestic violence?

In criminal law, two Latin terms *actus reus* and *mens rea* are important. "Actus non facit reum nisi mens sit rea" means "An act does not make a person guilty unless the mind is also guilty." In similar fashion, maintaining specific precepts can also be so identified since what we do is sometimes profoundly contrary to why we do it. Charity may be a precept in Islam, and charity is good, but we may give not for giving itself but to be adored, distinguished, and celebrated. Charity thus becomes a tool for the ego to maintain a social construct or persona where one thing is presented to the world but in the dark recesses of the heart and mind, the total opposite exists. So too can it be said of truth as truth can be used to create disharmony, conflict, and division to elevate someone and debase another with an agenda quite contrary to its supposed nobility.

From all outlined, precepts can actually serve to the detriment of individuals making them inauthentic, delusional, and unconscious. To willingly accept any precept without question is to also willingly surrender control of your life into the hands of another. Anyone who determines your precept is indirectly in control of your life since your precepts determine your thought processes, which determine how you act and live.

No longer can we afford to accept anything based on the authority of another or precedent. Diligent inquiry must now be our cornerstone as we recognize that there is no authority other than our soul. According to 2 Corinthians 3:5–6 (KJV),

> Not that we are sufficient of ourselves to think any thing as of ourselves; but our sufficiency is of God; Who also hath made us able ministers of the new testament; not of the letter, but of the spirit: for the letter killeth, but the spirit giveth life.
>
> The mind, which is generally very lazy and indolent, finds it easier to accept what someone else has said. The follower accepts "authority" as a means to achieve what is promised by a particular system of philosophy or ideation; he clings to it, depends on it and thereby confirms the "authority." A follower, then, is a second-hand human being and most people are completely second-hand. They may think they have some original idea but essentially, because they are conditioned to follow, to imitate, to conform, they have become second-hand, absurd human beings.
>
> —Krishnamurti, *The Impossible Question*[12]

---

[12] Krishnamurti, J, "The Impossible Question." Penguin Books 1978.

What Are Concepts?

> Intuition and concepts constitute … the elements of all our knowledge, so that neither concepts without an intuition in some way corresponding to them, nor intuition without concepts, can yield knowledge.
>
> —Immanuel Kant

Concept: a general notion, the immediate object of a thought," 1550s, from Medieval Latin *conceptum* "draft, abstract," in classical Latin "(a thing) conceived," from *concep-*, past-participle stem of *concipere* "to take in and hold; become pregnant," from *con*, plus combining form of *capere* "to take," from PIE root kap meaning "to grasp."[13]

Concepts are the foundation of all our thoughts. They can be considered the building blocks of all our ideas and beliefs, and they are created to describe, explain, and capture reality. There can be no cognition without concepts. Concepts do not exist in a vacuum and have no meaning on their own. Concepts are neither true nor false and may be even based on imagination and inventiveness. Concepts are ideas, the understanding of which requires utilizing further ideas to help explain and understand the original one, the essence of which at most times we are ignorant of.

Various theories exist as to how we establish ideas and conceptualize things and experiences that shape our development. In the field of psychology, four major theorists take center stage, namely

---

[13] https://www.etymonline.com/.

THE THIRD TESTAMENT

Eric Erickson[14] and his theory of psychosocial development, Jean Piaget[15] and his theory of cognitive development, Sigmund Freud[16] and his psychoanalytic theory, and Lev Vygotsky's[17] sociocultural theory. All these theories are diverse yet similar in many ways. Without utilizing psychological vernacular, basically, what these theories outline is that throughout our lives, we go through distinct developmental stages, and at different stages, diverse factors become more significant in the way we interpret or perceive our experiences and form and integrate ideas. Diverse factors involving nature and nurture play a critical role in this process, which occurs automatically and unconsciously.

So unconscious is this process that there are concepts and ideas we have accepted and integrated in our hearts and minds personally and collectively and we have not the faintest clue as to their origins. We have no idea who may have introduced them to us, from where they came, when they were assimilated in our consciousness, how it all happened, and what it means.

I remember as a teenager asking how the animals had gotten their names and was directed to Genesis 2:20 (KJV): "And Adam

---

[14] Erik Homburger Erikson (born Erik Salomonsen, 1902–1994) was a German-American developmental psychologist and psychoanalyst known for his theory on the psychological development of human beings.

[15] Jean Piaget (1936) was the first psychologist to make a systematic study of cognitive development. His contributions include a stage theory of child cognitive development.

[16] Sigmund Freud (1856–1939) was the founding father of psychoanalysis, a method for treating mental illness and a theory that explains human behavior.

[17] Lev Vygotsky, a Soviet psychologist, was the founder of an unfinished Marxist theory of human cultural and biosocial development sometimes referred to as sociocultural theory.

gave names to all cattle, and to the fowl of the air, and to every beast of the field; but for Adam there was not found an help meet for him." In hindsight, I recognize that throughout the years, I have shifted numerous times as it concerns accepting this ideology. I shifted from accepting without question that if God said it in the Bible, then it was so to wondering, *How could it be so with the existence of so many animals, especially when all were named on one particular day?* I later learned that time to us and time to God could be very different and that one day to God could be thousands of years to us. With that insight, I saw the possibility of Adam naming all the animals in one day.

Further along in life's journey in this era of advancement in science, I contemplated the possibility of God downloading in Adam's mind all he needed to know as was done with Keanu Reeves in the character Neo in the movie *The Matrix* where via a phone call, Neo gained the knowledge to operate a B-212 helicopter in minutes. In time, I recognized that Genesis 2:20 made mention only of the animals of the air and the land, so I started wondering about the creatures of the sea. Who then was responsible for naming the shark a shark, the salmon a salmon, and the octopus an octopus?

Without being sidelined and venturing into the issue of how the animals got their names, the point I am trying to make is to identify how we utilize ideas and concepts in shaping our perceptions and coming to conclusions and how they change as we change. Though I questioned certain ideologies over time, my foundational concepts, which were significant in shaping my thoughts, were never questioned. When and where did I accept the concept of God, especially in reference to Christianity and the Bible? What about the concept of God as espoused by Hinduism? Why didn't I consider or seek to find meaning or understanding from this framework? Such are the subtleties of concepts, which if they aren't observed direct our paths in ways we didn't necessarily choose.

These unconscious yet entrenched concepts and ideas establish our beliefs, shape our attitudes, and subsequently guide our behaviors. Our convictions on particular concepts have led to many judgments, conclusion, wars, and global conflicts. It is unfortunate that the validity of the foundation of our thoughts, our points of reference, and the guiding principles that direct all our decisions are not even considered in making decisions. We take for granted precepts and concepts that have been handed down to us whether directly or indirectly as judicial notice, and we function unconsciously without determining their accurateness or even their relevance in all the decisions we make.

My objective is to scrutinize some of the many concepts we adhere so as to gain understanding of their meaning that lays the foundation for many of our flawed conclusions, which guide our basic beliefs and mental structures, and which determine our worldviews.

Such rigid thinking perpetuated by conditioned and burrowed thoughts restricts freedom and establishes mental incarceration, albeit the incarcerated and enslaved are none the wiser of their state and position and unconsciously maintain it. According to a wise old lady, "If you wrote down the equation wrong, you may get a right answer but for the wrong equation." Are we ensuring that our equation is right so we can arrive at the right conclusion? Our intention here is to confirm that the equation is written having considered all possibilities and variables whether they be sociological, psychological, or spiritual as determinants, which would minimize the probability that the product does not require a solution itself.

> We are going to emancipate ourselves from mental slavery because whilst others might free the body, none but ourselves can free the mind.
>
> —Marcus Garvey (made popular by Robert Nestor Marley in "Redemption Song")

CHAPTER 2

SIGNIFICANCE OF CONTEXT

> The frame, the definition, is a type of context. And context, as we said before, determines the meaning of things. There is no such thing as the view from nowhere, or from everywhere for that matter. Our point of view biases our observation, consciously and unconsciously. You cannot understand the view without the point of view.
>
> —Noam Shpancer, *The Good Psychologist*

Context—"a composition, a chronicle, the entire text of a writing," from Latin contextus "a joining together," originally past participle of contexere "to weave together," from assimilated form of com "with, together."[18]

Words are much more than mere ink on paper or as some may say merely wind. Vibrationally and energetically, words are power (something we will explore later in this book), but from a physical perspective, they are symbols that represent something deeper and induce meaning. The meaning words induce stems from the symbolic context of the sociocultural and psychological framework from which all human understanding occurs.

---

[18] https://www.etymonline.com/.

Our failure to recognize the essence of these variables and their effects diminishes the capacity of what we are by design and serves as a detriment to our welfare and well-being. Seeing things in a fractured manner would ultimately perpetuate fractured behavior that would result in a fractured or broken society.

As with precepts and concepts, context is equally significant for holistic understanding and meaning. Context is defined as the parts of a written or spoken statement that precede or follow a specific word or passage usually influencing its meaning or effect. It is also the set of circumstances or facts that surround a particular event or situation. Many of us may have heard others stated before, "You have misinterpreted my remark because you took it out of context."

The media sometimes uses sound bites when quoting someone. If the broadcaster or media house fails to acknowledge the contextual framework of the speaker's words, or if there exists any ill intent or bias against the speaker, words espoused by the speaker may be edited to convey a message that totally contradicts what was intended. Occurrences such as these are identified particularly with politicians, especially around election times. It should be noted though that when deliberate utterances are made by persons who fail to recognize at the moment the detrimental consequences of such utterances, the meaning of what is stated is sometimes modified and readjusted by the speaker by simply redefining the context that changes the entire value of the speaker's words.

Those whom the police arrest are told, "You have the right to remain silent. Anything you say can and will be used against you in a court of law. You have the right to an attorney. If you cannot afford an attorney, one will be provided for you. Do you understand the rights I have just read to you? With these rights in mind, do you wish to speak to me?" In the United States, this preamble is known as the Miranda Rights.[19] Any experienced person in legal matters would always say that those faced with such situations should remain silent in the absence of legal counsel whether they are guilty or not since their own words as well intended as they may be can be detrimental if placed in the wrong context.

Context is categorized in six ways.

Situational

This context refers to the setting and environment in which we communicate. The manner in which we would communicate at a sporting event would be quite different from the manner in which we communicate at a funeral. Persons failing to maintain these unconscious and unwritten social mores would be automatically characterized.

The depths of situational contexts are far more reaching than that, though. At protest actions and riots, the mannerisms displayed by those involved are sometimes in total contradiction to how they normally are, a case in point being Rodney King as he pleaded for normalcy with his cry, "Why can't we all get along?" during the 1991 LA riots. His appeal, although the most reasonable at the time, was scorned even by those who weren't present since it was not conducive to the present context.

---

[19] Constitution of the United States, Fifth and Sixth Amendments. http://www.mirandawarning.org/originationofmirandarights.html.

Relational

All communication occurs in relationships, and the relationships themselves help define the communication and its meaning. Communication between father and son would differ from that between father and daughter as well as husband and wife. Communication between friends would also differ from the way they would communicate with strangers. Relational context defines not only the content of the message but its meaning as well. All social behavior takes place by definition in the context of a relationship, and relational context shapes not only social thoughts, feelings, and behaviors but also some seemingly nonsocial thoughts, feelings, and behaviors in profound ways.

Sociocultural

One of the most influential factors in meaning and communication has to do with the sociocultural context, which includes the historical context at any time. Sociocultural factors define and shape how people in a certain society think, feel, and interact with each other. These factors outline the social norms, beliefs religious and otherwise, opinions, moods, and attitudes of a society. Sociocultural context reflects the collective consciousness of a society whether it is individualistic or collective, whether it is materialistic or spiritual, and whether its members are egoistic or altruistic. These factors are the framework for their points of view that determine the way things are seen and identified.

Inner/Psychological

Fractured minds can see things only from a fractured point of view; hence, what they see would always be fractured though it would appear true to them. If we wear rose-colored glasses, that would color what we see and we wouldn't realize it. So it is with inner/psychological context. This contextual framework directs us to define and give meaning to things based on our inner states, desires, and values. Our personalities and archetypes (whether we are empathetic or narcissistic), our dysfunctionality, and our deficiencies (most of which are acute and of which at most times we are totally unaware) decide how we interpret and give meaning to things.

Symbolic

This context refers to messages that are primarily words that occur before or after a communication event that influence either the source or the receiver of the message or both in their actions or understanding of the event.

Physical

The physical environment natural and man-made may influence communication and our understanding. The painting of an office wall or its furniture type and placement immediately influences our thoughts and guides our behavior. This apparently simple physical feature has the potential to sway the minds of observers to an extent that automatically allows them to accept the office holder.

Lauren A. McDermott, a graduate student of Walden University, and Terry F. Pettijohn II, PhD, an associate professor of psychology at Coastal Carolina University in Conway, South Carolina, wrote a research paper, "The Influence of Clothing, Fashion and Race on the Perceived Socioeconomic Status and Person Perception of College Students."[20] It was presented at the twenty-third annual Association for Psychological Science Convention in Washington, DC. It proved that the type and brand of clothing and the race of college students were influential psychological factors in determining how they were perceived by others. The study showed that

> Models wearing the plain sweatshirt were judged to be most successful and important whereas models wearing the Kmart sweatshirt were judged to be least successful and important. Forms of prejudice and discrimination continue to influence our social cognitions and behaviors (Whitley & Kite, 2010), including perceptions of dress. Individuals make disparate judgments based on brand of clothing and class/race discrepancy.

This meant that persons who are dressed in a particular way as well as those of a particular race gained automatic approval from their peers. It also meant that this particular group had the power to send messages in whatever form, and whether such messages were

---

[20] Mcdermott, L. A. and Pettijohn II, T. F. "The influence of clothing fashion and race on the perceived socioeconomic status and person perception of college students". s.l. : Psychology and Society 4, no. 2 (2011), 64–75. http://www.psychologyandsociety.org/__assets/__original/2012/01/McDermott_Pettijohn.pdf.

accurate or not, the possibility of their being accepted by their peers was greater than that of those who did not dress that way or were from that particular race.

Similar cognitive and psychological influences occur when someone has a title such as Doctor or Reverend. Most unconsciously assume that such persons are authorities or experts and in some way are identified as being greater in understanding and intelligence than the rest of society is when that is not necessarily so. Because of this perception, such persons are more easily accepted and approved in the things they say and do even though what they espouse maybe flawed, inaccurate, and in some cases outright lies.

Notwithstanding the various contextual references in which a situation or information can be framed, no specific context exists in a vacuum. Numerous contextual frameworks function simultaneously, all affecting and influencing both sender and receiver via the written or the spoken word. Context is indeed of great significance since although one may consider all possible variables as they pertain to how ideas and concepts shape our thoughts, any given idea or concept taken without its specified context can convey a message totally contrary to the truth or the intention of the message.

From the etymological meaning of the word, it is clear that context entwines or integrates all aspects of any situation, circumstance, statement of content, or information to ensure a more holistic understanding. In spite of how content-filled a message may be, there can be no meaning without context. One might determine content from context, but context cannot be determined from content; content depends on context to give it life.

Information or knowledge of and by itself is of no real value, and though we have identified the importance of precepts, concepts, and context with reference to knowledge and communication, it is equally important in validating the content of the information or message in itself.

As a police officer, I was required to conduct numerous investigations and obtain accurate information, and I used various methodologies to do so. One such method was corroboration. For instance, if someone was arrested for an offense he claimed he could not have done because he was somewhere else at the time, I sought an independent witness or witnesses to corroborate that to establish the credibility of the statement.

I also had to validate the source of the information; was it a primary or a secondary source? Why did that person report it? That would unearth the agenda of the reporter again either validating or disproving the information.

We should be investigators where knowledge and information are concerned and especially as they pertain to our lives and existence. There are many things we accept and believe, some accurate and true while others are not. In many instances, fact and fiction, truth and deception are intermingled in a process called subterfuge, where one is unable to separate one from the other. As it is written in Matthew 24:24, we live in a time where if possible, even the very elect would be deceived.

How can we automatically accept all that we have been given from unquestioned or in many cases questionable sources or from sources that have a clear vile agenda? How can we accept uncorroborated and unverified knowledge? How can we speak with authority about something we are not knowledgeable of?

The fact that our parents, or another authority figure, or a popular person taught us something does not validate that something. Just because we read something doesn't mean it's true. The fact that a majority of people in society accepts or believes something does not validate or authenticate it.

I understand that there may be no way to possibly identify and know everything in its entirety—hence the notion of belief—but our beliefs should always be based on a sound and accurate foundation.

CHAPTER 3

THE POWER OF WORDS

> Words are singularly the most powerful force available to humanity. We can choose to use this force constructively with words of encouragement, or destructively using words of despair. Words have energy and power with the ability to help, to heal, to hinder, to hurt, to harm, to humiliate and to humble.
>
> —Yehuda Berg

We have seen how influential words are whether verbal or written relative to their content, concept, and context. Such however does not define the power of our words in whatever form inclusive of words never expressed verbally but internally as our thoughts.

Possibly thousands of books have been written on the subject; Dr. Cindy Trimm in her book *Commanding Your Morning*[21] directs readers to understand the power of their thoughts and words in shaping their lives and changing their circumstances. Dr. David Hawkins calibrated the frequency of words in his book *Power vs. Force*[22] showing how some words vibrate at low frequencies while

---

[21] Trimm, Cindy. "Commanding Your Morning." Charisma House, September 24, 2010.

[22] Hawkins, David. "Power vs. Force the hidden determinants of human behavior." Hay House, March 5, 2002.

others vibrate at high frequencies. In this chapter, I will show how the power of words is not limited to their content, concept, context, grammar, or syntax; they as symbols carry enormous power.

The origin of the word abracadabra appears to be ambiguous, it is however purported to be Aramaic in origin and means, 'what I speak is what I create.' Magicians and conjurors use it, and audiences consider it humorous. In medieval times though, abracadabra was an incantation used to ward off bewitchment and as a remedy for poor health. As fictional as the Harry Potter books and movies are, J. K. Rowling was not being fictional with most of the words used in the casting of spells including these.

> **Priori Incantatem** — the reverse spell effect, was derived in the following manner. "A priori" is a Latin phrase which means "from the earlier." This spell will cause the user's wand to regurgitate ghosts of its previously cast spells. "Incantatem" is derived from the Latin "incantare" meaning "sing or recite" — often used in relation to magic or witchcraft.

> **Homenum Revelio** — spell that tells you if humans are present from The Latin word "hominis" means "man," and "revelare" is the verb "to reveal." The spell will literally "reveal humans" if they are hiding nearby.

> **Sectumsempra** — curse which replicates slashing opponent with a sword. This spell is a two-parter. First, "sectum" is translated to "cut." And "sempra" (which you may recognize from the version of the

word used in the Marine Corps. motto "Semper Fidelis") means "always or constant." The spell's effect is an series of open cuts, and only the counter-curse can seal them shut. These and more were words used in the movie, which were all based on fact and not fiction.[23]

To understand the power of words, we need a basic understanding of our design as human beings as well as of our universe. The contemporary understanding in science is that nothing is as solid as it appears and that everything is energetic; this implies that everything vibrates. Vibrations have frequencies that can be measured in hertz and correspond with sound. Human beings can hear sounds of frequencies from about twenty hertz to about twenty-three kilohertz while dogs can hear frequencies of up to fifty kilohertz, the proverbial dog whistle.

Not being able to hear a frequency does not indicate that it has no effect on us since everything is energy and everything vibrates. We as human beings are electromagnetic by nature, and we vibrate at various frequencies based on our emotional states, thoughts, and consciousness and can be easily influenced and affected by frequencies. Without wanting to explain the way we are designed and how we interact and interface with everything in the universe just yet, let's stay focused on the power of words.

Because words have meaning, they evoke deep-seated thoughts, some conscious and some unconscious. Thoughts have consequences

---

[23] Renfro, Kim. "The real linguistic inspirations behind 13 'Harry Potter' spells." January 12, 2016. Business Insider, http://www.businessinsider.com/harry-potter-spells-latin-origin-2016-1.

so great that they determine our reality. Thoughts arouse emotions that share biochemical connections with our nervous, endocrine, digestive, and immune systems. This is where the concept of the mind-body philosophy arose, an ideology identified by some as new age and subsequently avoided.

Thoughts and emotions cause hormones to be released in the body such as serotonin, cortisol, adrenaline, and dopamine, and prolonged thought patterns can establish synaptic connections and neural pathways in the brain. Additionally, in understanding the epigenetic principle, our thoughts and emotions can actually send messages to our DNA influencing changes in the manner in which our genes express themselves. Let me summarize all this scientific jargon.

Research in the field of quantum science has unearthed that "invisible forces of the electromagnetic spectrum profoundly impact every facet of biological regulation."[24] Our entire biological state, i.e., our genetic structure, which includes all aspects of our cells and which are the building blocks of all our tissues, organs, etc., are affected by frequencies and energy, and our thoughts and emotions are energy. Our thoughts and emotions are responses or the products of our perceptions and beliefs; this functions in a sort of cyclic loop as thinking and feeling are in many ways reciprocal.

Certain thoughts perpetuate certain feelings, and certain feelings perpetuate certain thoughts. The more we think and feel in a particular way, the more grooves are established in our minds creating patterns that allows us to continue thinking along those paths and eventually form habits. Particular hormones are released

---

[24] Lipton, Bruce. "The Biology of Belief: Unleashing the power of consciousness, matter and miracles." Mountain of Love, March 1, 2005.

in our bodies as a result of these emotions, which further endorses what we feel and drives us to further think along those lines hence giving validity to what we believe that activated such thoughts. Such occurs whether what we believe is true or false. The continuous release of these hormones can also lead to addictions.

Words evoke thoughts and emotions; words can make us laugh, cry, and get angry. Words can put us in a contemplative state or in a state of fear and anxiety, all of which can and does have significant effects on all aspects of our being. Consider the power of the words of a good salesperson who convinces you to buy something you do not need. What about the persuasive command of a great attorney who convinced you that you're innocent of a crime you know you committed. Notice the phonetic similarity with spelling pertaining to words, and spells as it pertains to casting of spells and magic. Swearing is also known as cursing, to curse someone is not only identified with the use of derogatory language but a spiritual practice to bring some sort of harm to another. In both cases it involves the use of words designed to hurt or harm another.

We have briefly looked at the power of words, precepts, concepts, and contexts and how they direct our perceptions and beliefs and subsequently guide our thoughts and emotions, which shape our attitudes and behavior, alters our biology, and affects us in all spheres be they physical, spiritual, or energetic.

Many concepts and beliefs shape our perspectives and worldviews significantly. Some beliefs and convictions have led to global conflicts, wars, segregation, and perpetual suffering personal and otherwise. It is my objective to examine some of these concepts in a holistic manner that shapes and guides our worldview, beliefs, attitudes, and behavior and ascertain the foundation of these ideas. I hope that will allow us to reexamine our beliefs, see things from an entirely different perspective, and perpetuate a total shift in paradigm eventually raising the consciousness of society and ultimately establishing a better world for generations to come.

CHAPTER 4

THE CONCEPT OF GOD

> Man is a Religious Animal. He is the only Religious Animal. He is the only animal that has the True Religion—several of them. He is the only animal that loves his neighbor as himself and cuts his throat if his theology isn't straight. He has made a graveyard of the globe in trying his honest best to smooth his brother's path to happiness and heaven.
>
> —Mark Twain

It is perhaps apt that we continue our investigation of some concepts starting with a controversial one—that of God. The world's population is estimated at 7.6 billion, and 7 billion of them identify with a religion or with some superior force or power.

Christianity is by far the largest of the religions with over 2.42 billion adherents while there are about 1.6 billion Muslims around the world. The classifications are not that simple, however, since of the approximately 2.42 billion Christians, there are over 37 million churches in the world with over forty-three thousand Christian denominations worldwide.

The Catholic Church has the largest number of adherents estimated to be 1.285 billion. Protestantism, which is divided into the historical and the modern, is estimated at 920 million. Then there is the Eastern Orthodox Church with 270 million, the Restorationism and Non-Trinitarianism, which includes the Jehovah's Witnesses and the Church of Jesus Christ of the Latter Day Saints at 35 million ... the list goes on. There are significant theological and doctrinal differences between the main branches of Christianity.

Adherents of the faith usually propose that such differences in doctrine are minor and cite factors such as style and culture as factors responsible for such diversity. They stress that the essential and most significant element in Christianity is the belief in the salvation of Jesus Christ while everything else can be considered minor details. This is a failure to identify and to come to terms with the reality of the divisions that exist in the church on various doctrinal interpretations beyond the belief of Jesus Christ being responsible for salvation.

Many gays and homosexuals accept and believe in Jesus Christ as their savior but are still ostracized by the church due to their gender persuasions. This in itself refutes the notion that the division in the church is primarily due to such beliefs. Further, how can there be so much division when they are all guided by the Bible, which God allegedly inspired? Need I remind such adherents about the words of Matthew 12:25 (KJV), "Every city or house divided against itself will not stand," the very concept of denomination is not scriptural.

The decision to follow one church instead of another boils down to which one best suits you. The notion of religion and church is clearly based on subjectivity, on one's inclinations due to cultural beliefs and conditioning or possibly one's discontentment with another religion and not necessarily that of sound doctrine and truth.

THE THIRD TESTAMENT

When it comes to Islam, there are primarily three denominations—Sunni, Shi'a, and Sufi, and they have significant theological and legal differences with each other.

The following taken from the website onelittleangel.com outlines the branches and denominations of Islam.

Sunni

This fraction of Islam has the majority of followers which is approximately 90%, and is broken into four schools of thought. They are named after their founders Maliki, Shafi'I, Hanafi, and Hanbali.

Shia

If one were not a Sunni Muslim then more than likely they would be Shia. The Shia consist of one major school of thought known as the Jafaryia (referring to the founder) or the "Twelvers", and a few minor schools of thought, as the "Seveners" or the "Fivers" referring to the number of infallible leaders they recognize after the death of Muhammad. The term Shia is usually taken to be synonymous with the Jafaryia/Twelvers.

Sufism

This aspect of Islam can be best described as esoteric. Although most members of this sect can be identified with either denomination of Sunni or Shia, others are not from either denomination. The distinction here being based primarily on the schools of thought (madhhabs) are regarding "legal" aspects of <u>Islam</u>, the "dos" and "don'ts", whereas <u>Sufism</u> deals more with perfecting the aspect of sincerity of faith, and fighting one's own ego. There are persons who call themselves Sufis who may have never been a follower of Islam, or who may be perceived as having left <u>Islam</u>. There are also some, such as the Bektashi that are not easily categorized as either Sunni or Shiah, and then there is the Brelvi that can be categorized as both at the same time.

Another denomination which dates back to the early days of <u>Islam</u> are the Kharijites. Members of this group in the present day are more commonly known as Ibadi Muslims. A large number of Ibadi Muslims today live in Oman. Then there are the Wahhabis whose teachings consider several factors prohibited which are considered permitted in the four Sunni schools. There exist further sects of Muslims that are not generally accepted into the Islamic body such as, The Nation of Islam, The Ahmaddiya, The Druze, and the Zikris. Then there are religions such as the Baha'is, Babism and Sikhism which supposedly emanated from Islam but are considered independent and distinct.[25]

---

[25] http://www.onelittleangel.com/wisdom/quotes/islam.asp?level=4.

We have touched on only two of the major religions, Christianity and Islam, and have seen the diversity that exists within them alone. Other religious bodies give evidence of similar patterns of conflict and division, with each one claiming to be *the* one. It is not my objective to elaborate on what I consider the offshoots of a concept at the core of all religions but to investigate the concept itself, namely the concept of God, the one unifying factor they all share—the belief in a God.

There exists a world population of approximately 7 billion people who believe in or accept the notion of a God or gods in whatever name. This belief in God supersedes most if not all of their other beliefs and establishes precepts and principles that govern their lives and the lives of the generation that follows them. Whence did this concept derive? What does the word *God* mean? First of all, does God exist?

Those who do not believe in God will argue that the God concept is nothing more than a creation of humankind necessitated by the fact that people needed to find a higher power who could help them control their environments. Karl Jung took this concept even a step further by asserting that the specific nature of the God concept, which each individual eventually accepts, is nothing more than a collection of those qualities they lack.

Those who do believe in God will argue that the very creation around us is proof of God's existence. One of the famous arguments in this regard is known as the argument of Riley's watch. Riley was a famous philosopher who postulated his argument as follows: if a man went walking in the woods and stumbled upon a watch along the way, he might pick it up and investigate the way it operates. He might discover that the mechanisms inside the watch are incredibly complicated and that it effectively tells time by virtue of the fact that all its working parts combine successfully to calculate the passage of seconds, minutes, and hours.

If this person considered the possibility that the watch may have been formed by virtue of coincidental forces of nature, he would immediately discard that as impossible. He would reason that something as complicated as a watch must have been created by someone; that it must have had a creator. Following this line of reasoning, Riley asserted that the universe was far more complicated in its mechanics than a watch and must have been created by someone. The conclusion of Riley's argument is that God must've created the universe.

The purpose of this book is not to adjudicate the two positions—God exists or doesn't—but simply to stimulate thought, to shift you from simply accepting what you have been told for generations without question to seeking and establishing your own conclusions from a more informed and holistic position.

Many pubs in Ireland have plaques on the walls forbidding the discussion of politics and religion because such discussions can lead to differences of opinion expressed violently. This book will not have the final word concerning the existence of God, but that doesn't mean it shouldn't investigate the God concept itself.

Most people who believe in God do so because they have adopted their beliefs from their parents, environments, and cultures. Many are not certain about anything, but to be safe, just in case it is proven to be so, they confirm and accept something they truly do not understand. Similarly, those who do not believe in God often base their lack of belief on the fact that their own parents were not believers, or may have had some undesired experiences that in their perspective no God if there was one would have allowed, or having decided that the ideologies and dogma espoused for God's existence make no sense to them.

This is obviously an undesirable state of affairs, as all should investigate the question of religion and the concept of God for themselves, especially in view of the fact that it has such a great, overriding importance in life and twenty-first-century society. Today more than ever, international conflicts are often started by differences of opinion concerning the nature of God, and many wars have been fought exclusively along battle lines drawn in the sands of religious belief. The mere notion of engaging in or even contemplating war for whatever reason sheds light on one's overriding precepts, principles, and beliefs.

It isn't necessary to focus exclusively on some of the arguments I have raised here when you investigate the God concept. Even the most superficial of Internet searches will yield a wealth of arguments for and against the existence of God. A personal investigation of the God concept can improve your insight into the things you already believe in this regard and might help you change or amend some of the aspects concerning your point of view.

"But why should I spend any time doing this?" you may ask. "After all, I'm fairly happy with the way things are, and my beliefs concerning the existence of God don't really have an impact on my own life or the lives of those around me." But you would be one hundred percent wrong if you argued that way. We have already outlined the power of our beliefs and thoughts and how they ultimately direct our behavior and even influence our physiology and health. You might not think your beliefs concerning the God concept have an impact on your own life, but they definitely do. Our very existence is reflective of our beliefs and especially our beliefs about God, religion, and spirituality. Further, what foundation are we leaving behind for the generations that follow to build upon?

If you investigate your beliefs, you might discover that you need to make some changes to become more consistent in the things you do and the people and institutions you support. You may recognize that all if not most aspects of our beliefs, which shape and determine our lives, are based on mythologies, flawed ideologies, and fallacies that can hinder our life's purpose and restrict epitomizing our potential since we would have no true essence and meaning in our lives.

Another reason for evaluating the way you see the God concept is to not be caught off-guard when your children ask you one day to discuss this concept, and especially these millennials who would not simply accept something because it was so purported. You may be one of those I've already mentioned—someone who has simply adopted his or her parents' faith or lack of faith and doesn't want to merely transplant such beliefs on any child. There is nothing wrong in teaching your children to believe what you believe, but you should stress the importance of their investigating the matter themselves so they can position themselves accordingly in society.

We would now examine this concept from various perspectives allowing readers to have a more holistic view albeit not an absolute one. Many of us if asked would have a lot to say about God, about our love for him, about how without him we would be nothing, how in him we live and breathe, and the story goes on. If one is to make any adverse remarks about God based on the content of the statement, an automatic fear envelops us. An immediate reaction occurs within our entire autonomic nervous system, our adrenaline and cortisol levels increase, and a series of emotional effects occur including panic, fear, and anxiety. Such is the power and influence of a word we have ascribed a meaning to, a word that is symbolic and represents something, and that something is a thing we have not a clue about.

Somewhere along the historical time line, many factors became construed concerning the concept of God, worship, and the knowledge of self. I am sure that many of you have been a part of training sessions in which an exercise was done to show how information could be misconstrued from one person to the next in communication. A short message is given to one person in secret, and that person shares it with another, and the message is passed along until it returns to the person who started the chain. In almost every instance, the final message received was never the initial message sent, and this exercise involves only a few people in a possible ten-minute time frame. What then do you think may be the outcome of a message traversing diverse eras, cultures, and languages in a time frame spanning possibly millions of years?

Scientists recently announced the discovery of the oldest fossil skeleton of a human ancestor. The find reveals that our forebears underwent a previously unknown stage of evolution more than a million years before Lucy, the iconic early human ancestor specimen that walked the earth 3.2 million years ago."[26]

According to this *National Geographic* article, the human race is estimated to be over 3 million years old. Besides these aforementioned variables, there are several other factors for consideration including

---

[26] Shreeve, Jamie. "Oldest skeleton of Human Ancestor found." *National Geographic*, October 1, 2009, https://www.nationalgeographic.com/science/2009/10/oldest-skeleton-human-ancestor-found-ardipithecus/.

- The ignorance of people who in their darkened state lacked the ability or capacity to expound on that which was revealed prior to their existence at a time of enlightenment.
- The egotistical and personal agenda of fearful people who sought power and control and as a result deliberately destroyed and concealed truth from the masses to maintain their status.
- The agenda of the wise and the prudent who spoke in parables and left clues that only the diligent would unravel since the treasure and power that one attains in knowing the truth should be obtained only by the mature and disciplined and not the lazy, as it is said, "Tools in the hands of fools can be dangerous weapons."

I concur that there exists a higher power, a divine, conscious intelligence from which all existence emerged. I think that the word *God* and the concept espoused by society as it relates to that word restricts and limits this higher power and confuses and blurs the essence and divinity of all unseen forces.

Several variables attest to the existence of some higher, intelligent consciousness. What is not defined though is the state and form of such existence. No one can deny the order and precision that exists in all creation, an understanding gained from peering into space, from the observation of life on the planet itself, and of course the design and complexity of our bodies. The accuracy and precision allude to a designer, namely, God, which we identify as a noun. We however fail to consider that if there must be a designer, even the designer should also have a designer, and as a result, the recurring paradox would persist indefinitely. This trend of thought is of course a linear one and can be debated since the designer is not a part of the design and as such is not governed by its rules.

No one can deny the perfection with which the earth was designed. Its location in the solar system, distance from the sun, physical structure, and atmospheric conditions make it ideal for life as we know it. The earth's satellite, the moon, plays an integral role in oceanic currents and movement.

The design of the human being with its autonomic, sympathetic, and parasympathetic nervous system is still not fully understood. The workings of the brain and its various parts in conjunction with the mind, which is an intangibility, is still eons away from being grasped fully. It was only recently discovered that the heart radiates electromagnetic energy far greater than that which our brains radiate and as such is more potent than our brains.

An understanding of the code established in our DNA identifies a specific program unique to every individual. Discoveries about our quantum world and about how consciousness interfaces with wave frequency and collapses it into atomic particles are still in debate in the scientific world. It's as if we were not in the universe but were the universe, and all life is just fractions of a whole that work in tandem with each other.

I can continue to list numerous factors about our universe, our planet, and our beings that remain mind-boggling and reflect the notion of ultimate consciousness and supreme intelligence.

Defining God

The Merriam-Webster dictionary defined God in the following manner.

1 : the supreme or ultimate reality: such as a : the Being perfect in power, wisdom, and goodness who is worshipped as creator and ruler of the universe b Christian Science : the incorporeal divine Principle ruling over all as eternal Spirit : infinite Mind

2 : a being or object believed to have more than natural attributes and powers and to require human worship; specifically : one controlling a particular aspect or part of reality

3 : a person or thing of supreme value

4 : a powerful ruler

Most if not all these definitions we have heard before, but none identifies where the word itself emanates. What do we know about this word, its meaning, its history, or its significance? The word *God* throughout the scriptures had various meanings. When I say scriptures, I am not only referring to the Bible, which cannot truly be described as holy since holiness indicates unadulterated and untampered with, but I also refer to the Quran, the Mahabharata, the Upanishads, the Rig Vedas, the Bhagavad Gita, the gnostic texts, the Sumerian texts, the Egyptian Book of the Dead, and other ancient writings.

The Origin of the Word *God*

The exact history of the word *God* in Genesis 1 is unclear. The first time this word was observed was in the fourth century in the

Gothic Bible, which was contained in the Codex Argenteus,[27] where the words *Guda* and *Gub* were used for God. It was never used in any of the Judeo-Christian manuscripts, which were written in Hebrew, Aramaic, Greek, or Latin. Our best research revealed that the word *God* could be traced to Germanic and Indo-European origins, whereby a similar antecedent variation, *Hu*, was used, which meant "invoked one." Hu is Sanskrit in origin and meant to invoke the gods, a form that appears in the Rig Veda, one of the most ancient Hindu scriptures.

Does this mean that the word *God* itself stems from what can be described according to Christianity as having pagan origins? Whether we choose to accept this or not, all religious foundations have pagan roots. Who or what determines what is pagan, and what does pagan mean? Further, we would recognize that hu is actually the prefix of the word *Human*. If Hu transliterates to mean God and we are Hu-Man, does that imply that we are all gods who apparently exist in the form of humans? Accepting this ideology would understandably explain Psalm 82:6 (KJV), "I have said, Ye are gods; and all of you are children of the most High." And also, John 10:34 (KJV), "Jesus answered them, is it not written in your law, I said, ye are gods?"

Terminologies Used for the Word *God*

Various terminologies are used for this word *God* in the Old and New Testaments; some of the terms are Lord and Lord God, etc., yet we are told that they all refer to the same being. We are also told

---

[27] The Codex Argenteus is a sixth-century manuscript originally containing a fourth-century translation of the Bible into the Gothic language.

that God is the Supreme Being who is omnipotent, omnipresent, and omniscient and that all things exist as a result of him. Being a supreme being indicates that he is supreme among beings albeit a being. Being a being suggests conscious existence. In this case, personification has been implied as with gender since the word *God* infers masculinity as would the word *Goddess* imply femininity.

A Title—Not a Name

One of the first things we need to recognize is that the word *God* is simply a title and not a name, and from extensive research, it appears that diverse beings were afforded such a title throughout history and in various civilizations both from within our sphere and beyond the stars. Even in contemporary times, there are the law lords in the UK. According to Dictionary.com, Lord is defined as a person who has authority, control, or power over others; a master, chief, or ruler. Surely this definition does not indicate or even imply such a person as being all-powerful, omnipotent, or omnipresent. One of the first things we need to recognize is that the word *God* is simply a title, not a name.

Monotheism and Polytheism

The ideology of a singular God never existed in ancient civilizations. In Egypt, a myriad of gods or deities existed such as Ra, Anubis, Osiris, Isis, and Horus. The Greeks worshipped Zeus, Apollo, Aphrodite, Artemis, and the like. In Sumer, writings speak about the gods Anu, Enlil, Enki, Ninhursag, Utu, and others. And then the pantheon of Hindu gods is spearheaded by Brahma, Shiva,

Krishna, Vishnu, Hanuman, and Lakshmi, which are but a fraction. Whence did all these characters derive? Is it all fiction, fallacy, or mythology? Did one God possess diverse personalities and traits and was subsequently identified via the dominant characteristics in various cultures and civilizations? Or did many gods appear to different cultures and civilizations?

From this questioning emerges the incessant debate between monotheism and polytheism as scholars from both sides of the divide present convincing arguments to prove one over the other. As was highlighted in an earlier chapter though, once our concept is flawed, so would our conclusion be in spite of whatever data or research is added to the equation; hence, an understanding of this concept is required before we can begin to make sense of it all.

Monotheism is identified as the worship or reverence of one God while polytheism refers to the homage of many. Having many gods, however, does not imply polytheism, and paying homage to one God does not infer that there is only one as with henotheism. Numerous biblical references attest to the existence of many gods implied and expressed. This polytheistic view was the generally accepted concept of early humankind.

In Genesis 1:26 (KJV), we read, "And God said let us make man in our image and our likeness." The word *us* as a plural pronoun can be found in other passages, including Genesis 3:22 (KJV). After Adam and Eve ate of the forbidden fruit, God said, "Behold the man is become like one of us." In the time of Babylon, when the people were one and spoke and worked together as one, in Genesis 11:7 (KJV), God said, "Come, let us go down and confuse their language so they will not understand each other." Who was the us to whom God referred?

The word *God* in Genesis 1 translates to the Hebrew word *Elohim*, which appears over two hundred times in Genesis alone. As is the case with the word *God*, the root of this Hebrew word is highly uncertain, and it is a generic term rather than a specific name. The structure of the word itself is pluralistic in nature with Eloah/Eloh being the singular feminine form while its phonetic counterparts include the Aramaic word *Elah*, which is synonymous to the Hebrew *Eloah* and related to the word *Allah*. Yes, this is the same Allah as found in the Islamic Holy Scriptures called the Quran. From this exposition, the similarities between the God of the Bible and the God of the Quran are clearly observed if only by meaning alone. When one person says God and another says Allah, the difference stems only from dialect, not meaning.

The Plurality of God

There are quite a few theories about the use of the pronouns us and our and the use of the plural Elohim. One school of thought suggests that the grandeur and magnanimity of this God could be identified only with plurality; hence, the authors' choice of such words. Another theory proposes that the use of the plural pronouns is reflective of the three Gods, the Godhead, who were all present at the time of creation. Although they are three distinct presences, they are all one in essence. It is from this that the concept of the Trinity, the Father, the Son, and the Holy Spirit allegedly became established.

Concerning the first ideology, where it is gleaned that the magnitude of God is insufficient to be described using the singular noun and could have only been described using a majestic plural self, such form of writing is inconsistent with the writing style of the time, i.e., it is historically out of context. Further there are thousands of instances in the Bible where God used the singular pronoun referring to himself, yet on only four occasions did he use the plural pronouns in a majestic plural sense.

The Concept of the Trinity

The concept of the Trinity is not scriptural. The hypothesis of the Trinity wasn't validated until some three centuries after the time of Jesus Christ and the apostles, and it was debated for decades before that time. The roots of the Trinity concept originated in the dispute as to the exact nature of Jesus Christ, especially in relation to God, which was identified as the Arian controversy. This controversy involved primarily the concepts of three priests from Alexandria namely, Origen, Athanasius, and Aria and began about 318 and lasted until 381.

The religious indifferences that such concepts yielded meant great conflict and even death including Christians killing Christians. To attain religious and above all political control, the Roman emperor Constantine the Great convened the Council of Nicaea in 325 to bring to a close this Arian controversy. In a not so simple transition that lasted a few decades, the conclusion meant the establishment of the Nicene Creed. (This will be further explained in chapter 9, "The Christ Concept.")

The Nicene Creed[28]

We believe in one God the Father Almighty, maker of all things visible and invisible. And in one Lord Jesus Christ, the Son of God, begotten of the Father, only-begotten, that is, of the substance of the Father, God of God, Light of Light, true God of true God, begotten not made, of one substance with the Father, through whom all things were made, both those in heaven and those on earth: who for us men and for our salvation came down and was made flesh, and entered humanity and suffered, and rose the third day, ascended into heaven, is coming to judge the living and the dead: And in the Holy Spirit. But as for those who say that there was a time when He was not, and that before He was begotten He was not, and that He came into being from things that were not, or who affirm that the Son of God is of a different subsistence or essence, or created, subject to change or alteration, them the Catholic and Apostolic Church anathematizes.

As with the first theory, this ideology does not validate, justify, or clarify the plural pronouns used in Genesis to describe a single God. Scriptural references that theologians and biblical authorities use to validate that Jesus was indeed in the beginning in Genesis and involved in the act of creation with God include John 1, but with the wrong concept, it is understandable how one could form such a flawed conclusion.

---

[28] The Nicene Creed is a statement of belief widely used in Christian liturgy. It is called Nicene because it was originally adopted in the city of Nicaea by the First Council of Nicaea in 325.

John 1 states,

In the beginning was the Word, and the Word was with God, and the Word was God. He was in the beginning with God. All things were made through Him, and without Him nothing was made that was made. In Him was life, and the life was the light of men. And the light shines in the darkness, and the darkness did not comprehend it. There was a man sent from God, whose name was John. This man came for a witness, to bear witness of the Light, that all through him might believe. He was not that Light, but was sent to bear witness of that Light. That was the true Light which gives light to every man coming into the world. He was in the world, and the world was made through Him, and the world did not know Him. He came to His own, and His own did not receive Him. But as many as received Him, to them He gave the right to become children of God, to those who believe in His name: who were born, not of blood, nor of the will of the flesh, nor of the will of man, but of God. And the Word became flesh and dwelt among us, and we beheld His glory, the glory as of the only begotten of the Father, full of grace and truth. John bore witness of Him and cried out, saying, "This was He of whom I said, 'He who comes after me is preferred before me, for He was before me.

The Translation of the Word *Logos*

"In the beginning was the Word, and the Word was with God, and the Word was God." In the first instance, in many older translations including that of the original Greek texts, the word *Word*, meaning *logos*, was never capitalized; the capitalization was done with the intention of establishing personification, hence implying and subsequently transliterating the word *Word* with the word *Son*. This insertion, as simple as it appears, distorts the original meaning of this scripture and allows for the acceptance of dogma to justify the presence of a being with God in the beginning who according to the theologians happened to be Jesus.

Various scriptural references can attest to this insertion such as 2 Peter 3:5 (KJV), "For this they willingly are ignorant of, that by the word of God the heavens were of old, and the earth standing out of the water and in the water," Psalm 33:6 (KJV), "By the word of the Lord were the heavens made; and all the host of them by the breath of his mouth," Hebrews 11:3 (KJV), "Through faith we understand that the worlds were framed by the word of God, so that things which are seen were not made of things which do appear." Shall I go on? All the above scriptures reflect the creation story identified in Genesis, but *word* was not capitalized. This in my humble opinion is the word spoken of in the book of Genesis, not a man named Jesus.

We have all heard many quotes about someone's word being his or her bond, a reflection of his or her character. Numerous scriptures reveal that out of the abundance of the heart, the mouth speaks. James 3:2 (KJV) states, "For in many things we offend all. If any man offend not in word, the same is a perfect man, and able also to bridle the whole body." One's word is an expression of one's thoughts, and this was the logos. The perfection of this God expressed what he was by his word, whereby the purity, power and potency of this word caused waveform to collapse into particles from which his thought became manifest.

What did this expressed thought via word manifest?

And God said, Let the waters under the heaven be gathered together unto one place ..." And so it was. "And God said, let the earth bring forth grass, the herb yielding seed etc ..." And so it was. "And God said, let there be lights in the firmament of the heavens ..." And so it was. "And God said let the waters bring forth abundantly the moving creatures that hath life ..." And so it was.

Such was the power of the spoken word, a power we also possess since we too can speak to the unmanifest waveform causing it to collapse into particles known as atoms from which all things are formed; the difference however stems from our state of being. (This and more would be explored later.)

Let us continue with John 1 and the establishment of the dogmatic trinity concept devised with the intention of explaining the plural pronouns used in Genesis. John 1:3 (KJV) states, "All things were made through Him, and without Him nothing was made that was made." Here we see another attempt to distort the truth, of adjusting the map to fit the road. Various translations of the Bible that predate the 1611 King James Version fail to include the word *him* using instead the word *it*. This was discovered in seven of these texts including the Tyndale Bible, 1526; Matthew Bible, 1535;

Tavener Bible, 1539; Great Cranmer's Bible, 1539; Whittingham Bible, 1557; Geneva Bible, 1560; and Bishop's Bible, 1595 while the Coverdale Bible of 1550 used the words *the same*. When did *word* meaning *logos* transliterate to a *him*?

True Meaning of the Word *Logos*

The next question surely to follow would be based on John 1:14 (KJV), "And the Word became flesh and dwelt among us, and we beheld His glory, the glory as of the only begotten of the Father, full of grace and truth." Again, mistranslation based on a flawed concept would serve as the catalyst for one to erroneously perceive that Jesus was the one who was there in the beginning as the word was then made flesh. We have already established that the true meaning of the word *logos* was not Jesus but what was spoken by God. As a result, Jesus was also a manifestation of this spoken word and not the spoken word itself. The fact that he was described as the only begotten of the father is probably an indication of the manner in which he was apparently conceived. (The use of the adverb *apparently* was intentional.) Further, he was truly the expression of the essence of this spoken word since his life was a total embodiment of grace and truth. Indeed, the word had become flesh in Jesus yet Jesus himself did not preexist in the beginning as the word.

According to many Christian authorities, the fact that the plural noun was used with singular verbs and pronouns means that Elohim itself was singular. This is not so however in Genesis 1:26 (KJV), where God said, "Let us make man in our image, after our likeness." In Genesis 3:22 (KJV), after the man had eaten from the tree of good and evil, God said, "Behold, the man has become like one of

Us, knowing good and evil." Genesis 11:7 (KJV) reads, "Come let us go down there and confuse their language."

The plural nature of Elohim was confined, restricted, and manipulated in an attempt to make sense and fit the flawed paradigm of a God that supposedly existed alone in Genesis and other scriptures. Religious authorities have distorted and misconstrued the facts using syntax in language in some cases, while in others, they include personalities such as Jesus and the Holy Spirit in a Christian cornerstone concept titled the Trinity. This Trinity concept, which has no scriptural foundation, was established some three centuries after Jesus Christ primarily for political control. All of this was done in a bid to maintain power and ultimately make sense out of something that seemingly did not, at least in their present paradigm.

It is not my objective in this book to clarify or pursue word definitions, theological or etymological foundations, or historical data to prove this or that. My goal is simply to show how every aspect of our lives and subsequently our society, which is greatly influenced by our beliefs and thoughts, is at best without foundation. We continue to accept what has been handed down to us without question time after time to the point that mythology and lies have become jurisdictional and have gone beyond the fabric of our social lives and have become etched in our DNA and possibly our very souls.

Clearly, this generally accepted God concept is erroneous and difficult if not impossible for any free, right-thinking agent to accept. Does it mean though that there is no God? That there is no divine intelligence or divine, omniscient, omnipresent, omnipotent vibratory consciousness by which all things seen and unseen exist? No it doesn't, at least not in the implication of the word. It merely infers that this concept is a flawed one with various leaks and unsubstantiated claims that would make various scriptural references redundant and contradictory. Notwithstanding, acceptance of this concept would act as an obstacle and subsequently serve as a hindrance to the growth and development of most if not all of humanity.

A Fact about the Bible

Another factor we need to understand is that the Bible is simply a hodgepodge[29] of allegory taken from various cultures and texts throughout history. Aspects of Sumerian doctrine as recorded in the Sumerian texts,[30] the Hindu Vedas,[31] ancient Egyptian culture,[32] Greek mythology,[33] astrology, and otherwise can be identified in the Bible; the simplicity of the word *God* reflects this. According to Robert E. Detzler in his book *Soul Re-Creation*, "The Bible is 10%

---

[29] *Hodgepodge* or *hotchpotch* describes a confused or disorderly mass or collection of things; a mess or a jumble.

[30] Sumerian literature is the earliest known literature; it was written in the Sumerian language during the Middle Bronze Age.

[31] The Vedas are a large body of religious texts originating in ancient India. Composed in Vedic Sanskrit, the texts constitute the oldest layer of Sanskrit literature and the oldest scriptures of Hinduism.

[32] Ancient Egypt was among the earliest civilizations in Middle East and Africa. For millennia, Egypt maintained a strikingly unique, complex and stable culture that influenced later cultures of Europe.

[33] These stories concern the origin and the nature of the world, the lives and activities of deities, heroes, and mythological creatures, and the origins and significance of the ancient Greeks' cult and ritual practices.

history and 90% symbology."[34] Any attempt to unravel its contents in a literal and linear fashion would be impossible and would be a reflection of our dense, limited, three-dimensional, ignorant states. Trying to comprehend spiritual matters from a physical perspective is foolhardy. Only when one understands the quiddity and purpose of the Bible, its allegory and inter-dimensional nature, would one see beyond the letter and be guided by the Spirit. According to 2 Corinthians 3:6 (KJV), "Who has made us able ministers of a new covenant; not of the letter, but of the Spirit. For the letter kills, but the Spirit gives life."

---

[34] Detzler, Robert E. *"Soul Re-creation: Developing Your Cosmic Potential."* Spirtual Response Center, March 1, 1999.

CHAPTER 5

WHAT/WHO ACTUALLY IS THIS GOD?

Diverse beings were given the title of God in the scriptures because of their power, authority, and control; however, that does not imply they were the all-powerful creators of heaven and earth.

So what is this God really? I specifically ask what since God is beyond a who. This God we identify as the creator of all things is not a noun but a verb, a consciousness, not a creator. The first factor we need to acknowledge though is the word *God* and what it represents. We know that all words, although powerful, are symbols and represent something. We have already seen what the word itself means as well as its etymological definition. Further, according to David Hawkins, in consciousness frequency calibration, the word *God* calibrates at infinity, the highest vibrational state with words such as *virus* and *bacteria* calibrating at zero and one respectively. But what does the word *God* represent? To different cultures and persons of different demographics in various times in history, God represented different things. The ideologies perpetuated by early humans as to what God represented were more aligned with what God actually is than the modern views that pervade our mainstream culture. Before outlining my perspectives of the beliefs of early humans, I'll explore the contemporary views.

First, contemporary society has made God human but with supernatural powers. Whether we choose to consciously accept this or not, to most of us in contemporary society, God is male. The masculinity of this God is further revealed by the notion that he made man first while woman was merely an afterthought. Genesis 2:18 reads, "And the LORD God said, It is not good that the man should be alone; I will make him an help meet for him." Clearly the concept of reciprocity was not the motivation here; it was all about the man.

Notwithstanding, the downfall of the human race was based on the disobedience of the woman, who then misled the man, the head of the home. Various philosophical views are shared where this is concerned, all in an attempt to perpetuate some form of equality. If we were honest with ourselves, we would understand why legendary singer James Brown declared in 1966 that this was a man's world. Undoubtedly, if God isn't a man, the authors of this concept of God surely were, and this is so even though all life including Jesus comes from females.

Further aspects of God being anthropomorphized include but are not limited to the following.

- God has a face: "The Lord make his face shine upon you" (Numbers 6:25).
- God has hands: "You have a strong arm; your hand is mighty, Your right hand is exalted" (Psalm 89:13). From this scripture, it is clear that he is also right handed: "I stretch out my hand against Egypt" (Exodus 7:5); "He has stretched out his hand over the sea" (Isaiah 23:11).
- God has eyes: "The eyes of the Lord" are on the righteous (Psalm 34:15). And God keeps his eyes on the land (Deuteronomy 11:12).

- God has ears: "Incline your ear, O Lord, and hear" (2 Kings 19:16); "Let your ear be attentive" (Nehemiah 1:6).
- God has feet: "Thus says the LORD: 'Heaven is my throne, and the earth is my footstool" (Isaiah 66:1). For God to be sitting on a throne as outlined in Psalm 47:8, he must have a posterior too.

Some say God was anthropomorphized to allow humanity to be better able to relate to him since he cannot truly be understood by them. This notion, although it may have had a noble intent, is irreverent and has created numerous conflicts in the minds of many, especially when modern humans never had a true concept of God. How can we redefine what we never knew, to relate to what we never understood? Because we never had a true concept of God to begin with, the anthropomorphic perspective has taken root in our minds, which has caused us to confuse the omnipotent God with other gods.

We have entangled anthropomorphic aspects of a God that is not in any way human or even superhuman with other gods that were very powerful and had numerous humanistic characteristics. And because we never understood that there was a difference, or that the word *God* is simply a title and is plural in nature, we try using every imaginable justification to make sense of various scriptures that just could not make sense, especially in the concepts handed down to us. Our present mental schema could not assimilate certain glaring facts. So what do we do? We adjust the map to fit the road.

How could this God who we have been told is perfect have regrets? Genesis 6:6 and 1 Samuel 15:11 are two such cases where

God regretted doing certain things. In Genesis 6:6, he regrets making humans.

> And the LORD regretted that he had made man on the earth, and it grieved him to his heart. So the LORD said, "I will blot out man whom I have created from the face of the land, man and animals and creeping things and birds of the heavens, for I am sorry that I have made them."

In 1 Samuel 15:11, he regretted making Saul king.

> I regret that I have made Saul king, for he has turned back from following me and has not performed my commandments.

Let's be honest. Are these the utterances of an omnipotent, omnipresent, omniscient God who is perfect in all his ways?

Even Moses at one time had to reprimand God for the thoughts he had. Having been liberated from Egypt, Moses left the camp of the Israelites for a bit as he journeyed to the mountain to communicate with God. During his absence, the Israelites utilized their gift of choice and designed a golden calf to worship instead of God. We all know how jealous God can be (another humanistic trait), and as a result, God had intentions of destroying them all.

It was Moses who in his wisdom and empathy had cause to talk to God about what he intended to do, and he subsequently changed God's mind. Exodus 32:14 reads, "And the LORD repented of the evil which he thought to do unto his people." I can outline numerous other scriptures that show that this God spoken of in most of the scriptures is not the almighty God. We have confused the little gods with the big God, and as a result, we now do not have an idea of what is really the big G.

We acknowledge that God is Spirit, but then Spirit can take many forms. Even human beings are truly spiritual beings but are presently experiencing life from a physical perspective. We are not the only conscious life forms in the multi-universe; some have the ability to take on diverse forms inclusive of that of humans while some exist only in the etheric. Genesis 6, for instance, outlines a strange relationship between daughters of humans and sons of God: "And it came to pass, when men began to multiply on the face of the earth, and daughters were born unto them, That the sons of God saw the daughters of men that they were fair; and they took them wives of all which they chose." One would assume that the daughters of humans were the female offspring of human beings, but who were the sons of God who made these women wives? The story further states that children were the products of this union and that they were mighty and even giants. Many theologians refuse to acknowledge the essence of this since it is clearly beyond their scope of understanding and as such have outlined various possibilities in an attempt to invalidate such occurrences. Clearly, they were unaware of figures such as King Gilgamesh, who was identified as a demigod being two-thirds god and one-third human.

I'm not saying that these sons of God spoken about in Genesis 6:6 were angels, but numerous instances of angels taking the form of men are in scripture. Jacob wrestled with God in Genesis 32:22 and called the place in which they fought Peniel: "Jacob called the place Peniel, saying, 'It is because I saw God face to face, and yet my life was spared.'" Which God did Jacob see face to face? It could not have been the omnipotent, omnipresent, omniscient God, and if it was an angel as most biblical authorities proclaim, in this scripture, that angel was labeled God and translated as Yahweh. (We will explore this Yahweh later.) From the looks of it though, God got a darn good fight from Jacob.

Throughout the Bible, it appears that various entities were identified as God because of their power and ability, but in the essence of what we perceive God to be, these entities were not God. We need to acknowledge that in this boundless universe, we are not the only life forms, beings, or entities. Many of these beings whether defined as angels, demons, aliens, or otherwise have appeared to human beings of diverse cultures and demographics throughout history. The word *alien* was formed from the suffix *ali*, an Arabic word though mostly ascribed to males that simply means high or elevated. It means that anything that comes from the sky, or from high and does not belong to the earth can be classified as alien. A meteorite entering our earth's atmosphere would be classified as alien since it would be alien to earth. Visitors from abroad are considered aliens and illegal aliens if they are not here legally. The images of little green men we have been conditioned to accept by Hollywood as aliens is a far cry from what aliens actually are.

In Mali, West Africa, there exists an ancient tribe of people known as the Dogons,[35] who although not advanced in science and technology possess a wealth of knowledge of the cosmos and of creation. The Dogons had knowledge about the brightest star in the sky, Sirius, which is near Orion's belt and can be seen from the

---

[35] The Dogons are an ethnic group living in the central plateau region of Mali, in West Africa, south of the Niger bend, near the city of Bandiagara and in Burkina Faso. The population numbers between four hundred thousand and eight hundred thousand.

northern hemisphere in winter. Knowing about Sirius would not be considered something so spectacular; however, they were the first to indicate that the Sirius star has a companion star now known as Sirius B. Again, this may not be something considered spectacular, but Sirius B is invisible to the naked eye. Nonetheless, the Dogons, who were not astronomers and never had telescopes, knew about it.

They knew the density of this invisible star and that it rotated on its axis and had a fifty-year elliptical orbit around Sirius.[36] They knew all this since the thirteenth century, which was evident by artifacts discovered as well as a traditional ceremony done in celebration of completion of the stars orbit they call a Sigui. It wasn't until 1844 that the possibility of the existence of such a star was considered and not until 1862 that it was confirmed and seen with the introduction of high-powered telescopes. The Dogons also spoke about a Sirius C, a star that had a six-year orbit, something that contemporary astronomers have still not confirmed but may be able to as their telescopes and technology become more advanced.

This is but a fraction of what the Dogons knew. They knew about Jupiter and that it had four major moons, that Saturn had rings and that the planets orbited the sun. The Dogons knew all this before Galileo's time.[37] This is indeed very significant since most of our knowledge about the planets and our solar system are a result of Galileo's contributions to science. Even astronomers and scientists

---

[36] Sirius, also called Alpha Canis Majoris or the Dog Star, is brightest star in the night sky with apparent visual magnitude of −1.46.

[37] Galileo Galilei has been called the father of observational astronomy, the father of modern physics, the father of the scientific method, and the father of modern science.

of today are baffled by what the Dogons have presented. The big question though is how did the Dogons know these things?

The Dogons accredited a race of people called the Nommos for this information. The Nommos, which the Dogons called gods, were an amphibious race of beings that resided on a small planet that orbited Sirius C. They claimed that these beings descended from the sky in a vessel accompanied by fire and thunder and that they had been visiting earth for thousands of years.

For more information on the Dogons and the Nommos, I suggest you do some research yourself. What you may discover may be much more than you were taught. My only reason for mentioning the Dogons and the Nommos is to validate the fact that it appears that we are not the only conscious beings in the universe.

This story is not in the least an isolated one. Sumer, known as Iraq today, was identified as one of the earliest known civilizations. The Sumerians called themselves the black-headed people with the word Sumer, which is derived from the Akkadian language and meant "land of the civilized kings." The Sumerian people were noted for their architecture with elaborate construction, which resulted in the world's first cities such as Lagash, Kish, Eridu, Nippur, Uruk, and Ur. The biblical Abraham, identified as the father of many nations, was most likely a native of Ur before being told by Yahweh to migrate. The Sumerians were also skilled hydraulic engineers and developed complex irrigation systems. Their skill in engineering and architecture alludes to their mathematical ability. Our contemporary concept of time keeping of sixty seconds in a minute and sixty minutes in an hour is accredited to the Sumerians.

THE THIRD TESTAMENT

One of the most significant factors for which this civilization is noted for however is language. The Sumerian language,[38] which is identified as the oldest linguistic record, first appeared in archaeological accounts around 3100 BC. It was mostly replaced by Akkadian[39] around 2000 BC but held on as a written language in cuneiform for another two thousand years. It is in this language on tablets of clay that the ancient manuscripts identified as the kings' list was discovered. The kings' list is considered one of the most important and mysterious ancient texts ever discovered. It describes in great detail a time when earth was ruled by beings referred to as gods for thousands of years and offers details about numerous generations of kings who ruled over the land of ancient Sumer. The list gives their names and supposed lengths and locations of their kingships.

Besides the kings' list, the clay Sumerian tablets in cuneiform were discovered; many of them have not been deciphered. Some of these tablets include the Eridu Genesis, the Enuma Elish, the Atra Hasis, and the Gilgamesh epics. The contents of the deciphered tablets are mind-boggling. Various conflict exists among scholastic authorities, primarily between those who are pro Judaic/Christian and those who are not concerning the meaning of its contents.

> Eridu Genesis, in Mesopotamian religious literature, ancient Sumerian epic primarily concerned with the creation of the world, the building of cities, and the

---

[38] The Sumerian language was spoken in southern Mesopotamia before the second century BC and was the first language to be written in the cuneiform script.

[39] Akkadian was a Semitic language spoken in Mesopotamia (modern Iraq and Syria) between about 2,800 BC and AD 500.

flood. According to the epic, after the universe was created out of the primeval sea and the gods were born, the deities fashioned man from clay to cultivate the ground, care for flocks, and perpetuate the worship of the gods. Cities were soon built and kingship was instituted on earth. For some reason, however, the gods determined to destroy mankind with a flood. Enki (Akkadian: Ea), who did not agree with the decree, revealed it to Ziusudra (Utnapishtim), a man well known for his humility and obedience. Ziusudra did as Enki commanded him, and built a huge boat in which he successfully rode out the flood.[40]

The similarities between the biblical stories and those of the ancient tablets are strikingly profound and could shake the foundations of some of our beliefs. It is not my intention to identify to anyone what is true and what is not or to identify what one should accept. My intention is to simply encourage others to research diligently, read, absorb, find stillness, and allow the core of their beings to identify what is from what isn't. After all, truth cannot be told; it is only revealed. Truth does not come from without; it only comes from within.

It is in my view however, according to an old Caribbean saying "There is more in the mortar than the pestle," meaning there is more to this than meets the eye. If one is to accept the writings of the Sumerian tablets together with the story of the Dogons of Mali and connect that with the biblical story of Genesis, it would

---

[40] The Editors of Encyclopaedia Britannica. "Eridu Genesis Mesopotamian Epic." https://www.britannica.com/topic/Eridu-Genesis.

appear that this God known initially as Elohim in Genesis is indeed the Annunakis[41] spoken about in the Sumerian tablets. What this also means is that this God in Genesis is not the omnipotent, omnipresent, omniscient God we have been taught to believe in.

This understanding in my purview would explain why Adam and Eve could have hidden from God, who had to ask where they were. This would explain why Cain could have killed his brother Abel, and this supposedly omnipresent God, who had to have been present at the murder, observed Cain killing his brother and did nothing only to come after the fact and asked Cain, "Cain, where is your brother, and what have you done?" Religious adherents ascribe the actions of God to that of how we as human beings, being flesh and blood, would confront our own children when they did something wrong. This is despite their scripture, which indicates that God is not like men that he should lie (Numbers 23:19). If God was aware of Cain's killing Abel and still asked Cain for his brother when he knew that Cain had killed his brother, he was being deceptive in spite of all the ways such may be justified.

This would also explain the reason that when the people in Babylon were building a tower God had to come to earth himself to see what they were doing. Clearly he was not aware of what they were doing from where he was. I can quote biblical story after story and ask a multitude of questions anyone with a modicum of common sense, even a child, could ask, and that do not make sense, especially in the context in which we are taught. As was initially stated, we have confused these gods with God who is the source of all things.

---

[41] The name Anunnaki is derived from An, the Sumerian god of the sky. The name is variously written a-nuna, ^{d}a-nuna-ke$_4$-ne, or ^{d}a-nun-na, meaning "princely offspring" or "offspring of An."

Other Gods Found in the Scriptures

Yahweh is not the only God in the scriptures, as evidently many other gods existed. As previously mentioned, diverse beings were given the title of God in the scriptures because of their power, authority, and control; however, such does not imply that they were the all-powerful creator of heaven and earth.

One of the first notions we should contemplate is that the creation story did not occur in six days as we know days to be of twenty-four hours. The entire process may have possibly spanned eons with a day actually implying an era, which calculates at approximately twenty-four thousand years. There is a clear distinction between the God of Genesis 1 and the God of Genesis 2. From Genesis 1:1 to Genesis 2:3, the word used for God is Elohim; from Genesis 2:4, there is a shift from God to Lord God and from Elohim to Yahweh. According to Richard Elliot Friedman, the notion that the first five books of the Bible called the Pentateuch[42] or the Torah was written by Moses is a fallacy and that more than one writer was responsible for this section of the Bible and obtained data from diverse sources.

Christian scholars, in order to validate their God concept, would imply that the different names reflect different attributes of the one character since only one God supposedly exists. This ideology begs one to question the greatness of this singular God who continuously becomes jealous of other gods when there are supposedly no other gods for him to be jealous of. This is a God who instructs his free-will creation to have no other gods besides him even though he had given them the gift of choice.

---

[42] The word *Pentateuch* comes from two Greek words that mean "five books" or "five scrolls." According to tradition, the books were written by Moses.

Exodus 34:14 (KJV) states, "For thou shalt worship no other god: for the LORD, whose name is Jealous, is a jealous God."

Deuteronomy 6:15 (KJV) reads, "For the LORD your God in the midst of you is a jealous God; otherwise the anger of the LORD your God will be kindled against you, and He will wipe you off the face of the earth."

Psalm 79:5 (KJV) reads, "How long, O LORD? Will you be angry forever? Will your jealousy burn like fire."

In Deuteronomy 32:21 (KJV), he stated, "They have moved me to jealousy with that which is not God; they have provoked me to anger with their vanities: and I will move them to jealousy with those which are not a people; I will provoke them to anger with a foolish nation."

Clearly, the jealousy and anger expressed by God for the actions of people who failed to pay homage to him suggest that he alone wanted to be the focal point of humankind's attention.

Various scriptural references suggest that at times, people directed their attention to images be they graven or otherwise that lacked power and authority and thus could not do anything for them. Yet at other times, we see God making reference to other gods or entities that to him were not real.

Scriptural Proofs

- Leviticus 26:1: "You shall not make for yourselves idols, nor shall you set up for yourselves an image or a sacred pillar, nor shall you place a figured stone in your land to bow down to it; for I am the LORD your God" (idols).

- Micah 5:13: "I will cut off your carved images And your sacred pillars from among you, So that you will no longer bow down To the work of your hands" (idols).
- Exodus 20:4: "Thou shalt not make unto thee any graven image, or any likeness of any thing that is in heaven above, or that is in the earth beneath, or that is in the water under the earth" (idols).
- Deuteronomy 4:16–18: "Lest ye corrupt yourselves, and make you a graven image, the similitude of any figure, the likeness of male or female, The likeness of any beast that is on the earth, the likeness of any winged fowl that flieth in the air, The likeness of any thing that creepeth on the ground, the likeness of any fish that is in the waters beneath the earth" (idols).
- Jeremiah 13:10: "This wicked people, who refuse to listen to My words, who walk in the stubbornness of their hearts and have gone after other gods to serve them and to bow down to them, let them be just like this waistband which is totally worthless" (other gods).
- Judges 2:12: "And they forsook the LORD, the God of their fathers, who had brought them out of the land of Egypt, and followed other gods from among the gods of the peoples who were around them, and bowed themselves down to them; thus they provoked the LORD to anger" (other gods).
- Romans 11:4: "But what is the divine response to him? I have kept for myself seven thousand men who have not bowed the knee to Baal" (other gods).

Yahweh Is Not the Only God

We see that Yahweh is not the only God in the scriptures. He portrays himself as the God whom people should obey, but does that refers to all people or just to a particular sect, namely, the children of Israel? It is obvious from Judges 2:12 and various other scriptures that diverse sectors of humanity were paying homage to entities other than Yahweh.

In Egypt, the Pharaohs were doing fine serving the gods they had chosen until Yahweh decided to prove that he was stronger and sent Moses with a specific task he could have done easily were it not for God hardening the heart of the Pharaoh (Exodus 9:12).

In 1 Kings 18, the showdown between Elijah and the prophets of Baal undoubtedly reflects the existence of other beings, namely, Baal in this case. The story identified Yahweh as the indisputable winner; however, we are not certain about all the unseen variables involved in this showdown and whether the match was fixed.

The Limitations of Yahweh

Genesis 6:6 tells us that the all-knowing God had regrets about creating humankind; didn't he know beforehand what he was doing? How can one have regrets with awareness of the past, present, and future? In Exodus 32:14, even Moses had to reprimand God for what he thought to do, and guess what? God repented notwithstanding his egotistical display in Egypt simply to show Pharaoh who was the real boss in town. The lists of atrocities of this all-loving God who more than ever gives numerous commands to kill and who apparently loves the aroma of burnt animal carcasses is simply too much to comment on. His egotistical, haughty, angry, arrogant, indecisive, and above all confused personality leaves a lot to be desired.

Mistaken Identity

Christian authorities and adherents of the faith rationalize these circumstances in one way or the other with the view of showing that God is all who they think he is while ignoring the facts before them. In no way am I saying that God is not an all-powerful, all-loving, all- knowing being. I am saying that the God we have been taught to call upon is not. Research has unearthed that most of the beings we identify as God in the scriptures are not the all- powerful creator of heaven and earth. Indeed, they were powerful beings beyond the understanding of the average human being at that time in history with the capabilities of doing things that the ignorant would classify as miraculous. Here are some characteristics of this or these Gods.

They Accept Worship

One thing common among these gods is that they accept worship. Whenever Yahweh appeared and people worshipped him, he did not object. When he appeared in human form to Abraham, Abraham worshipped him. In various occasions in the Bible and Quran, when angels appeared to humans and humans attempted to worship them, they objected and reprimand humans for that. Though angels are also powerful beings, they don't accept worship at least not from us; the speculations as to why are numerable.

They Appear in the Form of Humans

They are not men or angels (Numbers 23:19), but they can appear in the form of man for a mission. The seemingly random appearance of Yahweh to Abraham was not an isolated occurrence. God had appeared to him a number of times previously (Genesis 12:7, 17:1–3, 22). These theophanies are not described in any detail, but they relate in a rather nonchalant, unspectacular fashion the idea that Yahweh descended from heaven to speak with Abraham (and then "went up" from him, Genesis 17:22). So in chapter 18, we are informed of another appearance of Yahweh to Abraham.

We are told that Abraham, while sitting in his tent, beheld three men approaching. Neither the Hebrew nor the Greek call them angels here but use common words for mortal humans. However, in Genesis 19:1, two of the men were called angels (or messengers in Hebrew and Greek). If two of them left for Sodom, then apparently, the third was left behind. He would seem to be the Lord, who remained speaking to Abraham in the last part of chapter 18.

They Are Powerful

They possess supernatural powers and can perform miraculous acts. Though they are powerful, apparently, they are not all powerful. Only the almighty creator God is all-powerful.

Which God to Choose

The point is that Yahweh is not the only God in the scriptures as evidently there exists many gods. So which God are we to choose?

In my assessment, we cannot until we find out a bit more about this concept not just with the meaning of the word but how and when the concept was established.

If the gods in scripture are not the omnipotent, omnipresent, omniscient God, who or what is? Who are they that we continue to identify with?

Subcontractors

These beings, many of which had their own agendas, can be identified as subcontractors who work under the direction of the all-powerful God to bring forth the physical realms. These beings made use of both the tangible and intangible in bringing forth various manifestations including the androgynous hybrid being in Genesis 2, which was further modified via genetic manipulation later on where the female aspect of this being was removed and established in a separate entity in the creation of a female supposedly called Eve.

Some of these gods even mixed with humans according to Genesis 6:4: "There were giants in the earth in those days; and also after that, when the sons of God came in unto the daughters of men, and they bare children to them, the same became mighty men which were of old, men of renown."

Such unions between god and humans would have obviously produced offspring, a product that would have been beyond the average human being. Products of these unions as previously mentioned included Sumerian king Gilgamesh,[43] the Greek hero

---

[43] Gilgamesh was a historical king of the Sumerian city-state of Uruk, a major hero in ancient Mesopotamian mythology, and the protagonist of the Epic of Gilgamesh, an epic poem written in Akkadian during the late second

Hercules, who was the son of Zeus and the mortal Alcmene, and Helen of Troy, a daughter of Zeus, and Leda, who was queen of Sparta, and many more. Although identified as mythology, the authenticity of these characters has evolved over time. For instance, the biblical strong man known as Samson and Hercules share many aspects. According to biblical commentator Adrian Clarke, "The conformity between these adventures of Samson and Hercules is self evident, and proves beyond a doubt that the fable of the one was composed from the history of the other."

Our Flawed Understanding of the Almighty Creator God

From the little that was outlined thus far, it is obvious that what we have been taught about God is flawed and unsound. Most of these beings whom we worship and identify as God are not the supreme, all-knowing, all-powerful, all-loving, intelligent, Grand Spirits responsible for the creation of this boundless universe. If we were to compare the facts to the structure of a government, most of these beings including Yahweh were ministers, not the prime minister.

Further, they all had agendas independent of human interests. Until we eradicate the indoctrinated fear that resulted from the acceptance of this false doctrine and erroneous concept, we will never be able to epitomize our highest potential. We would continue in maintaining this illusion as a result of the collective consciousness and maintaining our slave-like state that appears to be the agenda

---

millennium BC. He probably ruled sometime between 2800 and 2500 BC and was posthumously deified.

of an elite few. Let us now explore further as we seek to answer the question, If what we were taught was not the truth, what is?

According to Austrian neurologist and psychiatrist Victor Frankl, people must continuously search for meaning and understanding for their existence. From the earliest of times, humanity sought to find meaning and form an understanding of its existence. The fact of life on earth in its various forms and forces of nature, which are beyond their control, served as a catalyst for humans to acknowledge some thing or someone greater than themselves. In an effort, perhaps, to gain some kind of way to understand and manipulate these forces people started seeking a higher power, someone or thing might be able to assist them in gaining control over the forces of nature and other seemingly random powers.

Early humankind recognized numerous factors; they acknowledged that beyond this physical world existed an unseen world that apparently had some impact on the physical world. They also recognized the cyclic movement of life in the universe and as a result could foretell certain things. To better relate to these unseen factors, ancient humans personified these forces giving them physical characteristics. Before identifying these aspects of personification, lets us recognize the various classifications with which early humans sought to differentiate the spirit world.

The pygmies were one of the most primitive civilizations ever. Please note that the erroneous concept that we have conjured in our minds of the word *primitive* should initially be addressed. Taken from the etymological dictionary.[44]

---

[44] https://www.etymonline.com/.

'Primitive' - late 14c., "of an original cause; of a thing from which something is derived; not secondary" (a sense now associated with primary), from Old French primitif "very first, original" (14c.) and directly from Latin primitivus "first or earliest of its kind," from primitus "at first," from primus "first."

The contemporary ideology of primitive being not good and outdated is quite contrary to its meaning, especially in this context. Primitive meant prime, the first. From the word *primitive* comes the suffix prim—precise and proper. In recognizing the culture and practices of probably the most primitive civilization on the planet, we may get a more comprehensive and precise understanding of God.

Though primitive civilizations are considered barbaric and uncivilized, historical records, artifacts, and remains of these ancient people tell of an advanced civilization that was rich in culture and probably even superior to our contemporary society. Again, that is very much in contradiction to what we have been taught. A brief insight into ancient civilizations such as the Sumerian and Egyptian can validate such claims. So it was also with their spiritual life and the way they worshipped. We have been taught by historians and other authorities that these ancient people had many gods and that their religious practices were polytheistic and animistic. This ideology perpetuated by historians and theologians concerning the way these ancient people worshipped or acknowledged God was totally flawed.

Let's consider this for a minute. Today, as it is in our present time, scientists, historians, and other authorities are stilled baffled as to how the Dogons of Mali knew about the existence of Sirius B, its weight, and its fifty-year orbit among other things. Contemporary astronomers are yet to identify the existence of Sirius C, which the Dogons also spoke about. The grandeur of ancient Egypt up to now remains a mystery to our most learned scholars. According to Graham Hancock in his book *Finger Print of the Gods*, concerning the great pyramid of Giza,

> The northern face was aligned, almost perfectly, to true north, the eastern face almost perfectly to true east, the southern to true south, and the western face to true west. The average error was only around three minutes of arc (down to less than two minutes on the southern face)—incredible accuracy for any building in any epoch, and an inexplicable, almost supernatural feat here in Egypt 4500 years ago when the Great Pyramid was supposed to have been built.
>
> An error of three arc minutes represents an infinitesimal deviation from true of less than 0.015 per cent. In the opinion of structural engineers, with whom I had discussed the Great Pyramid, the need for such precision was impossible to understand. From their point of view as practical builders, the expense, difficulty and time spent achieving it would not have been justified by the apparent results: even if the base of the monument had been as much as two or three degrees out of true (an error of say 1 per cent) the difference to the naked eye would still have been too small to be noticeable.

On the other hand the difference in the magnitude of the tasks required (to achieve accuracy within three minutes as opposed to three degrees) would have been immense.

Obviously, therefore, the ancient master-builders who had raised the Pyramid at the very dawn of human civilization must have had powerful motives for wanting to get the alignments with the cardinal directions just right. Moreover, since they had achieved their objective with uncanny exactness they must have been highly skilled, knowledgeable and competent people with access to excellent surveying and setting-out equipment. This impression was confirmed by many of the monument's other characteristics. For example, its sides at the base were all almost exactly the same length, demonstrating a margin of error far smaller than modern architects would be required to achieve today in the construction of, say, an average-size office block. This was no office block, however. It was the Great Pyramid of Egypt, one of the largest structures ever built by man and one of the oldest. Its north side was 755 feet 4.9818 inches in length; its west side was 755 feet 9.1551 inches in length; its east side was 755 feet 10.4937 inches; its south side 756 feet 0.9739 inches. This meant that there was a difference of less than 8 inches between its shortest and longest sides: an error amounting to a tiny fraction of 1 per cent on an average side length of over 9063 inches.

Once again, I knew from an engineering perspective that the bare figures did not do justice to the enormous care and skill required to achieve them. I knew, too, that scholars had not yet come up with a convincing explanation of exactly how the Pyramid builders had adhered consistently to such high standards of precision.[45]

If contemporary scholars are at a loss concerning the mere physical infrastructure of these ancient civilizations, who were indeed primitive in the very essence of the word, and on what authority are they capable of defining the spiritual practices of these people? Yet they have formed conclusions from their limited perceptions and subsequently taught the world about the lifestyle and spiritual rites of a people whose physical contributions they are yet to understand.

If it is impossible to understand their physical infrastructure, their religious and spiritual practices would be even more incomprehensible. Topics of facts concerning these ancient civilizations, whose history, language, and writings, which includes cuneiform,[46] and hieroglyphs, which predate Aramaic, Arabic, and

---

[45] Hancock, Graham. "Fingerprints of the Gods: The Evidence of Earth's Lost Civilization." Three Rivers Press, April 2, 1996.

[46] Cuneiform is a system of writing first developed by the ancient Sumerians of Mesopotamia c. 3500–3000 BC. It is considered the most significant among the many cultural contributions of the Sumerians and the greatest among those of the Sumerian city of Uruk, which advanced the writing of cuneiform c. 3200 BC.

Greek, the language of the Bible and the Quran, are avoided and dismissed by both religious bodies.

Research on the pygmies revealed that they understood more than we were able to recognize. Their form of devotion or propitiation was threefold; they acknowledged the source of all things or the one great spirit being independent of all things and who was indefinable. They recognized the omnipotent, omnipresent, omniscient oneness of God as the ultimate creator and source of all. They also acknowledged God as existing in creation as well as the spirits of the ancestors. The manner in which they acknowledged all three varied. Albert Churchward in *The Origin and Evolution of Religion* expressed the spiritual custom of pygmies in the following manner.

> The One Great Spirit whom he cannot define or see, but to whom he erects a primitive altar and makes offerings, supplications, and invocations, and invents a sign or symbol to depict or imagine him objectively.
>
> He propitiates the Spirits of the departed by erecting little houses wherein he laces food, because he can see them and knows that they exist; not that he believes his former friends will eat the actual material food, but that the spirit of the food will be consumed by them and will satisfy their wants and thus they will leave him in peace.
>
> He propitiates the Elemental powers or spirits, but he does not believe that these are human, or ever had

> been human, neither does he believe that they are demons in the present day acceptation of the term. He recognizes them as a source or power, either for good or ill, and during the pre totemic period of human evolution he had not as yet imagined them by one or the other of the Zootype forms. These forms the later Nilotic Negro brought into existence to establish the distinction one from the other. He had no words to do so at that time, nor any other means to visualize and distinguish these elemental powers but by sign language.[47]

From this perspective, it is understood why all nature was revered and respected by early humans. Nature was God's expression; nature was also God. It wasn't that ancient people worshipped the rain, thunder, trees, and the buffalo; they acknowledged the God within them. It is in this vein that the question was posed in 1 John 4:20 (KJV), "If a man say, I love God, and hateth his brother, he is a liar: for he that loveth not his brother whom he hath seen, how can he love God whom he hath not seen?" Until we pay homage to the God that exists in all people, we cannot say we revere a God we cannot comprehend. How can we acknowledge and love the unmanifest when we cannot acknowledge or love the manifest?

We continue to see the consequences of a society that fails to acknowledge this concept. By failing to understand this concept, we fail to recognize the god in ourselves and everything else. As is written in Psalm 82:6 as well as John 10:34, "Jesus answered them, Is

---

[47] Churchward, Albert. "Origin and Evolution of Religion." Lushena Books, Bensenville, IL, United States, February 3, 2012.

it not written in your law, I said, Ye are gods?" This omission due to ignorance has led us to destroy our ecosystem, cause certain species to become extinct or near extinct, and made it relatively easy to hate another as we are unable to see God in each other and in all things. Accepting yourself as a god does not make you the Great Spirit. According to the Suni poet Rumi, "In form you are the microcosm, in reality you are the macrocosm."

Relative to the ancestral spirits acknowledged by the pygmies, such practices can be identified in numerous other cultures both ancient and modern. The fear that most of us may have about it is rooted primarily in our ignorance and endorsed by Western cultural conditioning. I am amazed at how many of us have had experiences that appear contradictory to what we have been taught. Because we have been conditioned to deny and doubt ourselves, however, we would prefer to accept what is told to us by those who may have never understood or experienced what we may have. When we explore the concepts of heaven and hell, life and death, and reincarnation, we expound on the essence of ancestral worship.

The concept of God as outlined by Western hegemony and perpetuated by orthodox Judeo-Christian-Islamic religions is inconsistent and above all flawed. God, the Grand Spirit, the source of all, the one indescribable and unfathomable, is without gender[48] yet encompasses male and female energies. These energies are expressed differently and do not necessarily refer to sex. The masculine and feminine energies in human beings are related to or identified with males and females albeit males and females both

---

[48] Gender refers to the socially constructed characteristics of women and men such as norms, roles, and relationships of and between groups of women and men. It varies from society to society and can be changed.

possess masculine and feminine energies. All of nature can also be identified that way, and so it is with the word Elohim, God in the book of Genesis.

The word Elohim is a plural noun that comprises the feminine and masculine noun and could be translated as god or goddess. Eloah is the prefix and is the feminine form of the word Elohim, while the suffix im is masculine by nature. For this reason, Genesis 1:27 reads, "So God created man in His own image; in the image of God He created him; male and female He created them." God's image is masculine and feminine; the word *God* could thus also be *Goddess*. The grand spirit can be described as androgynous[49] not from the perspective of personification but the energetic. Although individuality is a product of the Grand Spirit and within all aspects of individuality it exists, from its perspective, all things are one thing and the same thing albeit expressed differently.

All in All

The Grand Spirit is indeed omnipotent, omnipresent, and omniscient. All power is the grand spirit, and all power emanates from it. There is no place where the Grand Spirit is not. Yes, if there is a hell, God/Goddess would be there also. The Grand Spirit is the life of believers and atheists alike, of the angels and the devils.

The Grand Spirit is consciousness and energy and has always existed since energy cannot be destroyed but simply changes form. The Grand Spirit exists incorporeally and in physical manifestations. It makes up all that is, which means you are in essence the Grand

---

[49] Androgyny is the combination of masculine and feminine characteristics into an ambiguous form.

Spirit also. The Grand Spirit is in you, as you are in the Grand Spirit; this is why God is often referred to as the higher self. You are not separate from God/Goddess in this physical body. Your existence in fact depends on the continual focus of the Grand Spirit in the you with which you identify in this life. What most people have lost touch with is the axiom that God/Goddess evolves due to the thought born as a result of the physical life we are living.

God/Goddess gains omniscience through every thought that has ever been thought. This united consciousness that for communication's sake I call the Grand Spirit is in truth becoming conscious of itself through our every thought.

God/Goddess Is Everything

God/Goddess is everything around you. The Grand Spirit is your thought, your life, and your breath. The Grand Spirit is you. The immortal, the invisible and the only wise one is I Am Becoming. Most of us have ignorantly renamed the great I Am Becoming as the great I Am. Exodus 3:14 was transliterated, "And God said unto Moses, I AM THAT I AM: and he said, Thus shalt thou say unto the children of Israel, I AM hath sent me unto you," but that is a mistranslation. The great I Am Becoming Who I Am Becoming has been erroneously identified as a noun but is a verb. There is no difference between the creator and the created. All things are made by and of the Grand Spirit. All are the offspring of the Grand Spirit. All things seen and unseen, tangible and intangible are aspects or projections of the one God/Goddess.

The absolute cannot contain something that is not itself. If it did, it would not be absolute, the only one. I Am Becoming is the infinite process of evolution; it is all you are and all you will ever be. There is only one creative power, one source—the Grand Spirit; it is also called awareness, unconditioned consciousness, and life. There is only one life, and all things are made of life or consciousness.

The Unseen One

The unseen is made seen in manifested creation. It is never far from its creation; it lives in you and me; we are one in it. We are one with creative force for we are it. Apart from our flesh, there is no difference between us and it. God/Goddess is spirit, and we are truly spirit trapped in physical form. The most powerful force on earth is love, and the Grand Spirit is love.

People have always seen the earth and sky and their invisible qualities, their eternal power and divine nature, so they have no excuse for not knowing the Grand Spirit. Everything around you is a clear revelation of the infinite one.

In his book *Soul Creation*, Robert Detzler gave the best description of the Great Spirit.

> God is the Creative force behind everything, God is Creative Intelligence, Spiritual Life, Spiritual Substance, and Prime Mover of all that is. All of creations are imbued by God's life, substance and intelligence. We could say symbolically, that God is creative energy or the fire of creation. As the fire of creation, he is Light, a light far beyond our mortal understanding of the sun, the moon, the stars, and conventional light waves. The visible light that is

perceived by the naked eye is a lower vibrational state from the one great light that is over all and through all and is an expression of that which comes out of God. As Prime Mover, God creates only on a spiritual level by forming a consciousness the divine blueprint for that that would eventually become the formed or created heavens and the earth. It is for this reason that the scriptures indicate that everything was without form and void before creation.[50]

The Attributes of God/Goddess

- **Self-Existent**: God/Goddess has no cause; this divine pervasive intelligence does not depend on anything for its existence.
- **Transcendent**: God/Goddess is distinct from the universe as the carpenter is distinct from the bench.
- **Immanent**: Though transcendent, God/Goddess is present with and in the world.
- **Immutable:** God/Goddess is perfect in that it never changes nor can it change with respect to its being, attributes, purpose, or promises.
- **Eternal**: God/Goddess is perfect in that it transcends all limitations of time.
- **Omnipresent**: God/Goddess transcends all limitations of space and is everywhere.

---

[50] Detzler, Robert. "Soul ReCreation – Developing your Cosmic Potential," SRC Publishing, Lacey Washington, 1994, 7.

- **Omnipotent:** God/Goddess can do all things consistent with the perfection of its being. God/Goddess cannot do the self-contradictory (e.g., make a rock he cannot lift), nor can he do anything contrary to his perfect nature (e.g., he cannot change, cannot lie, etc.).
- **Omniscient**: God/Goddess knows all things including events before they happen.
- **Incorporeal**: God/Goddess has no body; it is an immaterial, infinite being of spirit.
- **One:** God/Goddess is a perfectly unique and simple being; there is therefore only one God/Goddess.
- **Morally Perfect:** God/Goddess is morally perfect in all respects.

God is not a noun but a verb.

CHAPTER 6

THE HISTORICAL JESUS VERSUS THE THEOLOGICAL CONCEPT

> The Gospels depict Jesus not as the man he was, but as the person the later Church desired him to be.
>
> —Rupert Furneaux

Here is another integral concept that subtly influences our lives tremendously. To many, Jesus is the answer for every problem though one may not even understand what the problem is. This belief goes beyond Christians and their adherents and includes non-Christians, who when in distress or disaster call on Jesus for relief since he is identified as the key to salvation, a unity with God after being delivered from sin and damnation. This is an objective only Jesus can fulfill with the notion and concept of sin itself being subjective and highly questionable.

Failing to accept Jesus means that one is doomed to hell. It does not matter what kind of life people may have lived, whether they were good, moral citizens helping the old and feeding the poor or whether they were thieves or murderers. All those who failed to accept Jesus as Lord would be confined to eternal anguish and misery in hell. This is in spite of the fact that human beings were allegedly designed as free-will human agents endowed with the gift to choose, yet if they fail to choose certain variables such as Jesus

Christ, their damnation would be never ending. What a Catch-22 if I ever saw one.

Several claims by believers and adherents of the faith identify how without Jesus, life would have been unbearable. Yet in total contrast, many have met their demises through death and destruction under the banner of Jesus. Christopher Columbus single-handedly decimated an entire nation of native people namely the Caribs and Arawaks in the Caribbean with impunity in the name of Jesus. Historical records reveal one of the culprits wrote: "So many Indians died that they could not be counted, all through the land the Indians lay dead everywhere. The stench was very great and pestiferous." The Indian chief Hatuey fled with his people but was captured and burned alive. As "they were tying him to the stake a Franciscan friar urged him to take Jesus to his heart so that his soul might go to heaven, rather than descend into hell. Hatuey replied that if heaven was where the Christians went, he would rather go to hell."

During the Inquisitions, thousands identified as heretics[51] and witches were burned at the stake in Jesus's name. Had I lived then, I could have met the same fate. In contemporary times though, the death sentence methodology is to kill one's character with propaganda via the mass media. Let us also not forget the slave ship *Jesus of Lübeck*,[52] which was one of the many ships involved in the Atlantic slave trade under John Hawkins, who organized four voyages to West Africa and the West Indies between 1562 and 1568.

---

[51] Heresy is any belief or theory that is strongly at variance with established beliefs or customs and in particular the accepted beliefs of a church or religious organization.

[52] In 1564, Queen Elizabeth I sponsored Hawkins by lending him her 700-ton *Jesus of Lubeck,* the first British slave ship to reach the United States.

The focus of this chapter is Jesus from a historical perspective as opposed to the theological narrative. Let's first explore the name Jesus, which according to adherents of Christianity is above all other names.

Much has been written about the meaning of the name Jesus by Christians and non-Christians. The fact that the letter *J* is not found in Greek or Hebrew and was included in the English language only in the seventeenth century allowed for a lot of interpretations as it pertains to translations, transliterations, and opinions of context in terms of tense and grammar. The spelling of the name Jesus has been applied historically for less than 400 years; it means that the character himself, if such a character ever existed, would not have even known that name. As a result, some sects argue that most call on a pagan god, namely Zeus rather than the Messiah, whose name in Hebrew was not Jesus.

The name Jesus used in English originates from the Latin form of the Greek Iēsous, a version of the Hebrew Yeshua, also having the alternatives Joshua or Jeshua. There were at least five other persons named Jesus in the Bible, namely Jesus Barabbas, who was the criminal whom Pilate released in lieu of Jesus; Jesus Justus, as identified in Colossians 4:11; Jesus, the son of Eliezer; Jesus, the Son of Sirach; and Joshua, which as stated earlier is an alternative form of the name Jesus. It is not my objective to play word games with this name since that is not the essence of this discourse. It was briefly outlined to show the impact and influence that this name has on the populace, but what do we really know or understand about this character other than what has been told to us for centuries?

The story begins with the Annunciation, when the angel Gabriel visited a very young woman perhaps just fourteen. Giving birth to a child may not have been any grand occurrence, but this child was the Son of God, or according to some perspectives, God himself. The story is that the young woman was surprised since she had never had sexual relations with a man, but the angel assured her all would be well and told her the name to give the child and his significance. This child would have been identified as a king who would save the world past, present, and future. This special young woman, the Virgin Mary, became pregnant without losing her virginity.

It is proposed that she gave birth to this child on December 25 in a manger in Bethlehem. For the past 1,700 years, the majority of Christian churches as well as other sects including Muslims and Hindus celebrate this day as Christmas Day. This date, however, is not mentioned in the Bible. Even prior to Jesus's alleged birth, nature worshippers and the like participated in various "pagan" rituals on December 25 that celebrated the rebirth of the sun having lain in a proverbial grave for three days at the start of the winter solstice, December 22.

On the night of the baby's birth, three kings, who were also known as the three wise men, bought the baby gifts of gold, frankincense, and myrrh after having followed a star that led them to the birthplace of the baby. From a young age, this child displayed gifts and abilities beyond the average young person's so much so that at age twelve, he could be found debating with the nation's greatest intellectuals.

This child became a young man and was baptized when he was thirty. He did miraculous things as he traversed cities and towns with his team of twelve men. Walking on water, healing the sick, allowing the blind to see, and raising the dead were just a few of his many feats. At age thirty-three, this alleged Messiah was condemned for a crime he didn't commit and was crucified. Crucifixion at that time was not uncommon, but his crucifixion was divinely meaningful since it was identified as a sacrifice, an act claimed to have been his primary purpose for being on earth—to die for the sake of humanity.

Though he was crucified and died, he was not killed. He consciously surrendered his spirit on his own accord and subsequently arose from the dead and later ascended to heaven, where he sits on a throne next to his Father, who had sent him. It is believed that Jesus will be returning to earth for his people.

There has been continual controversy concerning this apparent historical figure known as Jesus of Nazareth. Some say he had no historical existence and was simply a myth. This ideology has been known as the Christ myth theory, and it was first proposed by Constantin Francois Chasseboeuf de Volney and Enlightenment scholar Charles-Francois Dupuis. In 1793, Dupuis published the *Origine de Tous les Cultes*, a thirteen-volume discourse that identified Christianity and other religions has having astrological foundations.

The Christ myth theory was further recognized and perpetuated by many philosophers, authors, and authorities ancient and modern including Thomas Paine, W. B. Smith, G. A, Wells, and Robert M. Price. This theory proposed three basic arguments: the foundation of Christianity was pagan, there is no historical value in the New Testament, and non-Christian references concerning Jesus Christ dating back to the first century do not exist. Many scholars do not accept the Christ myth theory and believe Jesus did exist, but they do not necessarily accept the various historical events surrounding him. Hence, the argument for the existence of Jesus as opposed to his nonexistence is not that simple.

This contrast is what separates those who seek to simply study the historical Jesus as opposed to the historicity of Jesus. Historicity or historical authenticity is designed to separate fact from fiction. This mode of study pays attention to the systemic processes of social change and the social context of the authors as well as their intentions; it is designed to separate the subjective from the objective, fact from fiction. The objective of this holistic purview is designed to establish the truth concerning historical events thereby separating accounts that can be considered mythical from circumstances that are factual.

What most of these authors suggest is that there isn't much historical evidence for Jesus. How can someone be so influential and famous as Jesus was but with so little data as to his existence? Such dispute however is not confined to Jesus; the existences of many popular historical characters are questionable even now. One factor for this is the sociological context, where the oral tradition was the primary means of conveying messages.

Let's consider some historical figures whose authenticity and validity can also be questioned.

Homer

Homer was identified as the author of the Iliad and Odyssey.[53] There have been many questions about the actuality of Homer including his birthplace and the time he would have lived. Samuel Butler attempted to prove that Homer was actually a female. What little we know about Homer is incongruent with his status as a prominent

---

[53] The Iliad and the Odyssey are epic poems that describe the Trojan War, a conflict between the Greeks and Troy fought about 1200 BC.

writer of aristocracy in the Western world. According to award-winning author Adam Nicolson, "It's a mistake to think of Homer as a person but more as a tradition."

Pythagoras

Though he is considered the pioneer of mathematics, little is known of his mathematical achievements as there are no writings ascribed to him. Historical accounts of this character are almost nonexistent; he was identified as the son of the Greek god Apollo and had golden thighs. Pythagoras was deified and ascribed supernatural powers. The image representative of him in mathematical and geometry textbooks is not known to be his likeness. The popular geometric equation known as Pythagorean theorem and credited to him had been known by the Babylonians and Egyptians for thousands of years before him. Many consider him a myth given life by a religious group known as the Pythagoreans, who focused primarily on numerology.

Robin Hood

To many, Robin Hood was a heroic archer, a philanthropist who stole from the rich and gave to the poor during the mid-thirteenth century in England. This character was purely fictitious but was an archetype that reflected the mind-set of a population in a particular social context. Many characters even in contemporary times can be likened to Robin Hood, but he and his merry men were made up.

Santa Claus

A very popular character, especially with children around Christmas time, Santa is an obese, white bearded, Caucasian man who resides in the North Pole and who notes the deeds of children all over the world and distributes gifts to them via his sleigh pulled by reindeer.

This story is a myth based on a few historical facts. Saint Nicholas of Myra in Lycia, in Turkey, was a fourth-century Greek Christian bishop who was known for his generosity to the poor. One story held that he paid the dowries of three young women so they would not have to become prostitutes.

Many aspects of the Santa Claus story were derived from other cultures and times. Yule, for instance, from which Yuletide or Yule-time season was derived, is actually a Germanic event celebrated during the winter solstice. The Yule celebration as a whole was often referred to as "drinking jól" or yule. This term identifies that drink was an important part of the celebration, a notable aspect of the season even today. Numerous features of this Yule celebration were infused into the Christian Christmas concept including the ideology of Santa Claus.

The description of Santa Claus for instance with his long white beard was ascribed to the god Wodan also known as Odin and Jólnir, meaning Yule figure. This god led a ghostly procession through the sky, which was known as the wild hunt; from it, the story of Santa riding in the sky on his sleigh was derived.

Many factors can be identified from all that was outlined, but primarily that many of our beliefs and dogmas handed down through generations are not as clear cut and accurate as they are made out to be. So too is it with religious beliefs and concepts including characters such as Adam, Eve, Moses, Samson, and Jesus.

The era of the birth of Christianity was one of tremendous social upheaval and discord; the time from the death of Herod to the collapse of Jerusalem was a period of great rebellion and social chaos. The dates of Jesus's birth and death have never been identified, but from historical circumstances, it is known that he was born during the reign of Herod, possibly a few years prior to the death of Herod, and crucified during the reign of Emperor Tiberius and Roman governor Pontius Pilate since it was Pilate who sanctioned his death.

We know that Herod died in 4 BC, Emperor Tiberius reigned from AD 14 to 37, and Pilate died in AD 38. It is proposed that Jesus would have died around AD 33. Of all the evidence obtained as it pertains to Christianity, a great deal was a result of oral tradition that lasted over fifty years until there were writings on the subject. The majority of information concerning Jesus and Christianity is derived from the four Gospels and the writings of Paul, namely, the Acts of Apostles. Concerning the four Gospels, however, none existed prior to AD 70 and were based on oral tradition.

As a result of this and other factors, an incessant debate persists concerning the authorship of the Gospels. Some say they were not written by eye witnesses or by those whose names the Gospels bear. If we were to reflect on the writings of Paul, although much may be gleaned about Christianity, the same cannot be said for a figure who was as prominent and controversial as Jesus and on whom the entire basis of Christianity is allegedly established. Paul has been credited as the greatest of the apostles having written the most books in the Bible, but his references to Jesus are few. According to Barrie A. Wilson, professor of humanities and religious studies,

York University, Toronto, "If We Only Had Paul, What Would We Know of Jesus?"

Many scholars question the existence of Jesus; though I accept his existence, in many ways, I do not. I am convinced that such a character did exist as historical evidence suggests as little as it may be. However, I believe that most of what was written or suggested about him is not necessarily so and that many aspects of pagan tradition that existed prior to the Christian era in diverse cultures as well as other factors were infused and incorporated into his life and existence and peddled as historical fact, which in itself distorts the truth. Hence my differentiation between the historical Jesus as opposed to the theological one.

One of the reasons why some refuse to identify Jesus as a true historical figure is related to various other personifications that existed prior to his existence and that bear striking similarities to what we are taught about Jesus. Many Christians may outright dismiss what I am about to outline, but I hope they can reconsider what they have been taught, consider what may be presented, do some research, and seek to make sense out of what is real. In many cases, we have been misinformed by flawed ideologies, dogmas, and concepts.

It can be difficult to accommodate what we do not believe. If we believe that Adam and Eve, the first humans, were created by God about six thousand years ago, how do we accept the discovery of the fully formed, erect, skeletal remains of a *Homo sapiens* female found in Ethiopia that carbon 14 data proves to be over 3.5 million years old? We can question the notion of Adam and Eve being six thousand years old, which is not based on any substantive data, and accept the scientific discovery, which is based on empirical research. Here, I am simply presenting research and facts.

Of the sixty-six books of the contemporary Bible, although everything is expected to be surrounding Jesus to the point that it was also prophesied about his coming in the Old Testament, only Matthew and Luke present details of Jesus's birth, and even they are not consistent with themselves or the historical record.

Matthew 1:16 reads, "And Jacob begat Joseph the husband of Mary, of whom was born Jesus, who is called Christ." Luke 3:23–38 also outlined the genealogy of Jesus whereby Joseph was again identified as a descendant in this lineage and as the father of Jesus. Outlining this lineage was very significant since it was prophesied that Jesus the Messiah would come from the lineage of David, to which Joseph belonged. In comparing and examining both genealogies of Matthew and Luke, however, clear inconsistencies and contradictions are unearthed; for instance, in the genealogy of Matthew, Joseph's father was Jacob while in the genealogy of Luke, his father was Heli.

The paternity of Jesus identified through the descent of Joseph in Matthew and Luke was to fulfill biblical prophecy since Jesus was supposed to belong to the lineage of David the tribe of Judah. If the Holy Spirit had impregnated Mary, why trace Jesus's lineage through Joseph, who is not his biological father?

Theological scholars, in a bid to justify this apparent conflict, state that the genealogy of Jesus as outlined in the narrative of Luke was that of Mary since it is clear that Joseph was not Jesus's father. This is a case of shifting the road to fit the map since nowhere in scripture is Mary's lineage mentioned. Why or what give biblical scholars the idea that Luke outlined the lineage of Mary? At that time in history, the father, not the mother, determined a child's lineage. Numbers 1:18 (KJV) states,

> And on the first day of the second month, they assembled the whole congregation together, who registered themselves by families, by their fathers' houses, according to the number of names from twenty years old and upward, head by head.

Circumstantial evidence does not validate this claim aligning Mary with David. Mary was identified as the cousin of Elizabeth, the mother of John the Baptist. Elizabeth was a descendant of the high priest Aaron, which aligns her with the tribe of Levi, not David. As a result, Luke could not have proposed the lineage of Mary in chapter 3 bringing her in line with the seed of David. For argument sake, let's still say that this is what Luke did; it would mean that Heli was Mary's father and subsequently Joseph's father-in-law. There is nothing in or out of scripture whether historical or contemporary that validates such.

The scriptures and history do not tell us who Mary's parents were. She was described only as pure and holy even though she gave birth to the Savior. What an exemplary role model she could have been if more were known about her.

Eastern churches including the Catholic Church identified her parents as St. Joachim and St. Anne based on traditional and apocryphal writings such as the Protoevangellium of James,[54] written around AD 150. Such writings, however, were never placed in the

---

[54] The Gospel of James, also known as the Protoevangelium of James or the Infancy Gospel of James, is an apocryphal gospel probably written around AD 145, which expands backward in time the infancy stories contained in the

scripture, and though the writing style was similar to scripture, it was never identified as divinely inspired and accepted as canon.

Could it be that the popular ideology of Mary being conceived of the Holy Spirit in the context that was taught for generations is flawed and that Joseph did indeed impregnate Mary? After all, even Paul in Romans 1:3 stated, "Concerning his Son Jesus Christ our Lord, which was made of the seed of David according to the flesh." Seed as we know refers to sperm, and the seed of David according to the flesh refers to the lineage of Joseph; this thought would certainly be aligned with the genealogy as proposed by Matthew and Luke. It is suggested that at the time the apostle Paul wrote this scripture, the dogma of Jesus being born of a virgin had not yet been promulgated.

Matthew 1:23 identify the birth of Jesus as the fulfillment of prophecy: "Behold, a virgin shall be with child, and shall bring forth a son, and they shall call his name Emmanuel, which being interpreted is, God with us." It is purported that such was in conjunction and the fulfillment of the prophecy of Isaiah 7:14: "Therefore the Lord himself shall give you a sign; Behold, a virgin shall conceive, and bear a son, and shall call his name Immanuel."

The word *virgin* in Isaiah was derived from the Hebrew word *Alma*, the meaning of which has been the cause of much contention for centuries. According to Wikipedia,

> **Almah** (עַלְמָה 'almāh, plural: 'ălāmōṯ עֲלָמוֹת) is a Hebrew word for a maiden or woman of childbearing age who may be unmarried or married. It does not, in and of itself, indicate whether she is a virgin, for

---

Gospels of Matthew and Luke and presents a narrative concerning the birth and upbringing of Mary herself.

which a different Hebrew word betulah is used. The Septuagint version of the Old Testament renders both Hebrew words almah and betulah as the same Greek word parthenos. The term occurs nine times in the Hebrew Bible.

Thus, the virginity of Mary was not necessarily based on the state of her hymen, sexual purity, abstinence, or chastity but on her age. Mary was a young woman of childbearing age who had not yet given birth and who might or might not have been a virgin. Mary's supposed virginity comes into question, as does the ideology of the fulfillment of the prophecy. This is one of the many reasons that various sects including some Jews refuse to accept Jesus of two thousand years ago and still await the coming of the Messiah.

Could it be that Mary conceived in the natural way and that a divine, advanced soul with a particular predisposition was subsequently infused into this zygote in her womb, a soul with a set agenda and ability to epitomize and make manifest his potential in the flesh? The Greek word for virgin in the sense of Hebrew almah and betulah is parthenos, from which the word parthenogenesis comes. Parthenogenesis is the production of an embryo from a female gamete without any genetic contribution from a male gamete. The concept of parthenogenesis was commonplace in ancient times among diverse cultures; thus, the ideology of female reproduction without the involvement of a male was not a novel idea as is suggested in the biblical nativity narrative.

Is it possible that same was done to the Mary and Jesus story as was done to the Santa Claus story? That fact and fiction were combined, and features from diverse cultures and times in history were merged and incorporated so as to make the story as it is?

Historical research tends to validate the idea that concepts taken from various pagan cultures were infused not only in this birth of Jesus story but also throughout the Bible. Various images, statues, and figurines of a mother holding a child in her arms and sometimes to her breasts identified as the Holy Mother or the Mother of God representative of Mary holding the baby Jesus and commonly known as the Madonna and Child can be seen throughout history well prior to the time of Mary and Jesus.

Christianity was birthed at a time and in a region where the ideology of virgin birth and Mother of God were commonplace. Over sixteen thousand years ago, Mutemua was identified as the virgin queen of Egypt and was said to have given birth to the pharaoh Amenkept or Amenophis III, who was responsible for the construction of the temple of Luxor. An entire nativity scene was inscribed on the temple. In a temple at Denderah in Egypt dedicated to Hathor, in the chambers known as the Hall of the Child in his Cradle, the figure of the virgin mother giving birth to her child of light can be seen.

The Egyptian god Ra was said to have been born of the virgin mother Net or Neith and had no biological father. Isis, wife of Osiris and mother of Horus, was also identified as the mother of ancient Egypt and worshipped as a virgin mother. Her son Horus was said to be a parthenogenetic child and identified as a Christ figure. Various Egyptologists and other scholarly authorities have compared Horus with Jesus and suggest one story was borrowed from the other.

Numerous statues of Isis breastfeeding Horus and Mary and baby Jesus can be seen even today in several places in the world including the Louvre, the Metropolitan Museum of Art in New York, and in the British Museum. This Mother of God figure can be seen in numerous cathedrals such as the Chartres Cathedral and all over Europe including Sicily, Spain, and Switzerland, and Turkey, Africa, India, and the Caribbean. In many instances, the image stands alone minus the child and is dark in complexion hence referred to as the Black Madonna. In Mexico, she is known as the Lady of Guadalupe. Some in India refer to her as Kali Mai, while in Trinidad, she can be found in the La Divina Pastora Roman Catholic Church in a place called Siparia. The title La Divina Pastora means Divine Shepherdess. According to the Encyclopedia Britannica, "This statue of the Virgin Mary is venerated by Roman Catholics as well as by Hindus, who see her as a manifestation of the goddess Kali and call the statue Siparee Mai or Mother of Siparia." Even indentured Chinese laborers who came to Trinidad identified the statue as Guan Yin, their East Asia goddess of maternal compassion. In 1795, Pope Pius VI established the Catholic feast day of La Divina Pastora, the Holy Shepherdess.

This does not exhaust the list of the many mythological females who gave birth to a divine being and who were identified as virgins. Mithra was a Persian god and a remodel of the Vedic god Mitra, who was born of a virgin. Aditi was known as mother of the gods. In some school of thought, he was identified as being born of a rock; this equates however with being born of the earth. In Greek cultures, the earth was personified and identified as female and known as the goddess Gaia. The ancient mother of the gods Cybele was also regarded as Mountain Mother, and the title means rock or mountain. Cybele was sometimes identified more than a mother goddess but also as a virgin with her consort Attis.

In India, Devaki can be seen with her divine baby Krishna suckling her breasts in similar fashion to the blessed virgin and child. Perictione, the mother of Plato, was considered a virgin and was conceived via an immaculate conception. Dionysus, the son of Zeus from the virgin goddess Persephone, was said to be born of a woman and of God. Inanna/Semiramis, virgin mother of Sumerian/Babylonian god Dumuzi/Tammuz ... and the lists goes on.

In his book *The World's Sixteen Crucified Saviors*, Kersey Graves compared the stories of the birth, death, and life of sixteen figures (who all predated Jesus) with the accounts of Jesus and found astonishing similarities; they were not identical, but the author showed that the elements of Jesus's story were not uncommon.

Other writers give credence to the work of Graves. Dorothy Milne Murdock has written extensively on the topic: *The Christ Conspiracy: The Greatest Story Ever Sold, Suns of God: Krishna, Buddha and Christ Unveiled*, and *Christ in Egypt: The Horus-Jesus Connection*.

The legitimacy of the birth of a child known as Jesus by a female identified as a virgin by the name of Mary has been rejected by numerous authorities. This belief has been classified as a religious myth and was subsequently added to the doctrine of Christianity in the late first century AD. It is proposed that one of the many reasons such was done was to establish Christianity as superior to the various pagan religions in the Mediterranean region at the time. As such, a demigod or God himself was required to manifest in the flesh to overshadow any prior dogma of a similar nature, and the character identified as Jesus became that figure.

No specific date was identified for the birth of Jesus in the Bible, but December 25 is celebrated the world over as his birth date. There has been much controversy concerning the accuracy of this date; some believe Jesus could not have been born on that day. However, Jesus's nativity is of critical importance in the Christian calendar since it is used as an indicator for a period prior known as Advent or the Lent of St. Martin. Historically, the church acknowledges six specific periods namely Advent, Christmas, Epiphany, Lent, Easter, and Pentecost, all of which surround Jesus.

Advent, which means "coming" in Latin, is the beginning of the Western liturgical year and commences on either the fourth or sixth Sunday before Christmas. This concept was initially introduced at the Council of Tours of 567 and was intended as a preparatory period for the second coming of Jesus while commemorating the first coming. During this time, adherents of the faith were required to prepare themselves by fasting at least three times per week, an order declared by Bishop Perpetuus of Tours.

Clearly, if December 25 was simply symbolic and just a celebratory day primarily for children as implied by most adherents, the six church periods that include Advent would also not be significant since these momentous periods are all synchronized with the birth of Jesus being identified as December 25.

Matthew and Luke are the primary sources concerning Jesus's birth. According to Luke 2, Jesus's birth coincided with the taking of a census. Joseph and a pregnant Mary had to travel to Bethlehem since Augustus Caesar issued a decree that a census be taken of the entire Roman world.

> And it came to pass in those days, that there went out a decree from Caesar Augustus that all the world should be taxed. (And this taxing was

first made when Quirinius was governor of Syria.) And all went to be taxed, every one into his own city. And Joseph also went up from Galilee, out of the city of Nazareth, into Judaea, unto the city of David, which is called Bethlehem; (because he was of the house and lineage of David:) To be taxed with Mary his espoused wife, being great with child.

According to Luke, this was the first census to have taken place while Quirinius was governor of Syria (Luke 2:1–3). Matthew on the other hand failed to identify any census being done at the time, which would have been the reason Joseph would have taken his pregnant wife on a journey to Bethlehem. What Matthew did mention in 2:1 however was Herod, who was supposedly the king at the time of birth of Jesus: "After Jesus was born in Bethlehem in Judea, during the time of King Herod …" Matthew also indicated that Herod in a bid to execute baby Jesus, who was touted to be king, had all babies under two years slaughtered in a horrendous event known as the Slaughter of the Innocents. As significant as such actions may have been at the time, there are no historical records that validate such an occurrence. The biography of Herod the Great was extensive; early historian Josephus wrote two books on the life of Herod. Historically, Herod was an astute and successful politician; however, in his later years, he seemed to have suffered some sort of paranoia.

Some of his recorded atrocities include putting to death one his wives (Mariamne) and his mother-in law even though Mariamne was allegedly his best wife. He also had three of his sons killed on suspicion of treason, and he killed other family members including uncles and cousins. Clearly this description of Herod identifies a man with the disposition to kill babies. The biggest question though was why wasn't anything documented in reference to this event? Could it be that Luke simply was unaware of this occurrence even though something as significant as this should have gained national interest? Or could it be that such an event never occurred? Of course as it is said in the theological world, absence of evidence is not evidence of absence. If indeed the Massacre of the Innocents never occurred, ascribing such activities to someone like Herod would have definitely been very shrewd taking his known activities and character into question.

This however is not the only thread of evidence albeit circumstantial that questions the circumstance. In Luke, a census took place in AD 6, when Quirinius was governor of Syria. An intelligent guess would indicate that Jesus would have been born around that time since Joseph and Mary journeyed to their hometown, Bethlehem, for the census, and that was where Jesus was born. Matthew wrote that Joseph took Mary and Jesus to Egypt to escape Herod having been warned of the danger in a dream.

Something in this story appears amiss though. Historically, we know that Herod ruled for thirty-four years from 37 BC to his death in 4 BC, yet the census occurred in AD 6, ten years after Herod's death. It is either there was no census or no Herod. If there was no census, why did Joseph and Mary go to Bethlehem? If there was no Herod at that time, there could not have been a Massacre of the Innocents. It has been purported that the story of the census was created to place Jesus in Bethlehem to fulfill the prophecy in Micah 5:1–2, the bearing of which is also questioned. Notwithstanding, the story of Moses in Exodus bears characteristics strikingly similar to the Massacre of the Innocents where, like baby Jesus, Moses as a baby was placed in a basket in the river to avoid being slaughtered and who in similar fashion to Jesus ended up in Egypt. Even this can be explored further; however, sufficient information has been shared that will allow you to come to your own conclusion.

CHAPTER 7

A BRIEF HISTORICAL PERSPECTIVE

The historical and theological Jesus became confused. It seems that the philosophical and theological perspectives and arguments had much influence in society during this time in history. As a result, an understanding of the sociological and historical cultural context at the time is exceedingly significant.

Prior to Jesus and until after AD 70, the region of Palestine and particularly Judaea was in a state of turbulence. The Jews were under Roman dominance for quite some time, from the installation of Herod the Great as king until his death in 4 BC. The situation only escalated after his son Herod Archelaus took over the throne after his father's death. After ten years of tyranny and misrule, Archelaus, who was exceedingly unpopular with the Jews, was deposed by Rome, and Judea was incorporated into the Roman Empire with a procurator in control. The council of seventy-one, the Sanhedrin,[55] which was controlled by the high priest and the Sadducees,[56] had a minimal degree of authority since nothing of significance could be done without the approval of the procurator.

---

[55] The Sanhedrin was an assembly of either twenty-three or seventy-one rabbis appointed to sit as a tribunal in every city in ancient Israel.

[56] The Sadducees were a sect or group of Jews that was active in Judea during the second temple period starting from the second century BC through the destruction of the Temple in AD 70.

The Jews abhorred foreign domination while maintaining specific ideals that they were God's chosen people. They earnestly expected a Messiah who would liberate them from the clutches of Rome and eventually lead them to global control; that was the premise of the nationalistic movement, which was at the forefront of social upheaval. The continued adversity and suffering under foreign rule served as the impetus for the Jews to desire the immediate appearance of their Savior, the Messiah. This desperation led to a number of Messiahs being identified between 4 BC and AD 135. Some of these Messiahs included Judas of Galilee; Theudas, who headed an insurrection against the Romans; Eleazar, son of Deinaeus; Jacob, who was tried by the Sanhedrin; Menahem, son of Judas of Galilee; Jesus of Nazareth; and the final revolt of Simon ben Kosevah in AD 132.

The historical context is critical in recognizing Christianity as it is known today, which includes the theological Jesus and the concept of Christ. The collapse of Jerusalem in AD 70 included the destruction of the holy city and the temple. It meant the annihilation of the Jewish national cause, the obliteration of the apostolic leadership, and an end to the Nasoraean Messianist movement. Most important, it also meant a shift in the paradigm of the doctrine perpetuated by the historical Jesus and his original followers and the introduction of the doctrine of the self-appointed apostle Paul.

Though Paul never knew Jesus personally, his rise to prominence was his Damascus road experience. The basic ideology of Paul as it pertains to the identity of the Messiah was in many ways syncopated with prior pagan mythologies. For instance, the ideology of Jesus being God in the flesh, a demigod, or some divine being was never taught by Jesus or his early followers and not even accepted by the early Jews. To the Jews, God stood alone; any other belief would have been blasphemous. Even the doctrine of the trinity was not accepted by the Jews. The idea of Jesus being a demigod, since he had not been conceived naturally, was not a new concept as was outlined previously but a borrowed concept Paul attributed to Jesus.

Jesus appeared focused on an agenda related to the Jews alone. His mission seemed to be local, not global. The Jews then were waiting for a prophesied Savior to liberate them from Roman subjugation. Jesus was one of the many figures so identified; hence, his role was primarily a political one at least according to the Jews. He was to be a man, a Messiah, a Savior filled with the spirit of God and equipped with the ability and skill to lead the Jews, supposedly God's chosen people, to overcome the Romans and gain global domination.

Many biblical scholars contrasted basic principles outlined by Jesus to those of Paul, where it appears that Paul spoke quite contrary to Jesus. In Matthew 10:5–6, Jesus instructed his disciples, "Do not go in the way of the Gentiles, and do not enter any city of the Samaritans, but rather go to the lost sheep of the house of Israel." In Matthew 15:24, Jesus responded to the Gentile woman who sought his help, "I was sent only to the lost sheep of the house of Israel." Paul on the other hand declared in Romans 11:13, "But I am speaking to you who are Gentiles. Inasmuch then as I am an apostle of Gentiles, I magnify my ministry."

Jesus identified the kingdom of heaven as Israel's prophetic earthly kingdom; Matthew 4:17 reads, "From that time Jesus began to preach and say, "Repent, for the kingdom of heaven is at hand." And Matthew 6:10 reads, "Your kingdom come. Your will be done, On earth as it is in heaven." Paul's definition of the kingdom of heaven was based on the heavenly position of the body of Christ; 1 Corinthians 15:50 reads, "Now I say this, brethren, that flesh and blood cannot inherit the kingdom of God; nor does the perishable inherit the imperishable," and Romans 14:17 reads, "For the kingdom of God is not eating and drinking, but righteousness and peace and joy in the Holy Spirit."

Differences also identified Jesus focusing on the law while Paul dealt with grace; Matthew 5:17–18 reads, "Do not think that I came to abolish the Law or the Prophets; I did not come to abolish but to fulfill. For truly I say to you, until heaven and earth pass away, not the smallest letter or stroke shall pass from the Law until all is accomplished." In Matthew 7:12, we read, "In everything, therefore, treat people the same way you want them to treat you, for this is the Law and the Prophets." Paul's focus was not on the law even though he knew the law having been born under Mosaic law,[57] but his emphasis was on grace as identified in Romans 6:14–15: "For sin shall not be master over you, for you are not under law but under grace. What then? Shall we sin because we are not under law but under grace?" and Galatians 5:18, "But if you are led by the Spirit, you are not under the Law."

I could identify many more perceived discrepancies between Jesus's words and Paul's words. Their messages were definitely not the same, but they can be compared to water and ice. Ice is denser than water, but H_2O constitutes them both.

Many contemporary theologians and biblical authorities have issues with Paul, and back then, he received grave opposition from Jesus's disciples with his view being rejected by the apostolic leaders

---

[57] Mosaic law primarily refers to the Torah or the first five books of the Hebrew Bible.

at Jerusalem. As a result, Paul's doctrine was not accepted and gained prominence only after the collapse of Jerusalem and about twenty years after he died in AD 64. Paul's views and doctrine became the cornerstone for Christianity, a new global religious agenda that began as a Jewish messianic movement hinged on Jewish nationalism. As a result of the sociological and cultural contexts, this doctrine of Paul once rejected and disapproved became Christianity's main principles.

Could it be that the Jews never understood Jesus's purpose? Could it be that just as John the Baptist presented a shift in the paradigm, Jesus established a path or prepared society for something even more evolutionary that Paul propagated? If true, it means that this in and of itself shows that nothing is static, that consciousness continues to evolve more and more into wholeness, and in the same manner that it didn't end with Jesus, neither did it end with Paul.

Christianity's greatest expansion and development, however, began in the third century in a chaotic Roman empire of failing institutions and diverse religious beliefs. According to Rupert Furneaux in his book *The Other Side of the Story*, "From a mere 50,000 in the third century, Christians numbered a tenth of the total population of the Empire, a hundred million, by the middle of the fourth century."[58] Clearly, Christianity deviated from its original design perpetuated by the historical Jesus and became a viable commodity in shrewd Constantine's mind.

In a move many considered miraculous, Constantine, emperor of the west, and Licinius, emperor of the east, signed a letter popularly known as the Edict of Milan in February AD 313. This decree was

---

[58] Furneaux, Rupert. "The Other Side of The Story." (Cassell & Company, London, 1953).

allegedly designed to embrace Christianity since Christians were apparently being persecuted for their monotheistic beliefs; the decree allowed for religious tolerance since there existed various religious beliefs at the time. As acceptable and fair as it may appear, this event had far-reaching consequences politically, sociologically, and otherwise. Christianity was accepted, and the state started to lend support to the church and incrementally became more involved in church affairs from the building of churches and the printing of Bibles to the point of establishing church doctrine.

The notion of separation of church and state, a phrase coined by Thomas Jefferson in a letter he wrote to the Danbury Baptist Association of Connecticut in 1801, was totally nonexistent at this time in history. Such a separation of church and state ideology was and is presently contradictory and a total misnomer since the foundation of all religious doctrine was established by the state. It means that whatever you decided to believe was already altered and designed by the state and subsequently directed to be accepted by an ignorant society. As a result, the need for the state to get involved in any contemporary matters involving the church is minimal since the state had already laid the foundation of our religious beliefs.

This Edict of Milan came on the heels of severe persecution under Emperor Diocletian known as the Diocletianic[59] or Great Persecution in 303. It is perceived that the persecution of Christians at the time was simply based on their monotheistic religious beliefs;

---

[59] The Diocletianic or Great Persecution was the last and most severe persecution of Christians in the Roman Empire. In 303, the Emperors Diocletian, Maximian, Galerius, and Constantius issued a series of edicts rescinding Christians' legal rights and demanding that they comply with traditional religious practices.

however, when taken in context, the nature and extent of such persecution were not as simple as identified. Why were Christians singled out in a society that had so many diverse philosophies? An understanding of the history of the messianic movement from which the Christian ideology was birthed (albeit assimilated with concepts of diverse cultures and a shift in its original agenda), there were sound reason to be cautious of Christians.

Christians at that time in similar fashion to some sects of contemporary Islam would have identified any non-Christians as infidels. They were considered antisocial by most of society, not civil minded, and as a result, they were gravely unpopular with most of society. The pious and peaceful demeanor of turn the other cheek promoted by Christian literature was not reflective of their historic background. Jesus's directive to his disciples in Luke 22:36 was, "But now, he that hath a purse, let him take it, and likewise his scrip: and he that hath no sword, let him sell his garment, and buy one"; it identifies a perspective to which little attention is paid. We see in John 18:10 where Peter drew a sword and severed the ear of a Roman soldier, "Then Simon Peter having a sword drew it, and smote the high priest's servant, and cut off his right ear. The servant's name was Malchus." Civilians were not permitted to carry weapons in Roman-occupied territory; it was a capital offense to be found with one.

Ten major periods of persecution were identified in the early church beginning with Nero. Contrary to popular opinion though, Nero didn't persecute Christians because of their religious beliefs but because they were identified as being responsible for the great fire of Rome, July 18, 64. This fire that allegedly lasted for nine days affected ten of Rome's fourteen districts and totally wiped out three. It is from this that the popular legend of Nero fiddling while

Rome burned was coined, but this legend was of course fictitious, especially since the fiddle didn't exist then.

The final and most severe persecution of Christians occurred in 303 under Emperors Diocletian, Maximian, Galerius, and Constantius. A series of edicts rescinding Christians' legal rights and demanding that they comply with traditional religious practices was issued.

Although the Edict of Milan was declared, there was still no central or governing authority for the church, and various conflicts continued to pervade. The conflict about the nature of Jesus continued to be an issue over the years and continued well into the fourth century. Diverse perspectives shared by Arius and Athanasius, priests in Alexandria, captured the attention of the empire. Arius, like many in his time, refused to equate Jesus with God and indicated that the son was subject to the father, that, "The son had a beginning but God alone is without beginning." Athanasius on the other hand proposed the contrary and indicated that the son and the father were of same substance and were one; he coined the nonscriptural term *homoousion*[60] to mean such.

This debate captured national attention that came to the notice of Emperor Constantine, who subsequently invited 1,800 bishops to an ecumenical council (318 attended) to quell this conflict in the Christian body. The Council of Nicaea (325) was the first of many ecumenical councils over the years designed to establish church orthodoxy and doctrines. Arianism, the nature of Christ, the celebration of Passover, and the ordination of eunuchs were

---

[60] Homoousion is a Christian theological term most notably used in the Nicene Creed for describing Jesus as the "same in being" or "same in essence" with God the Father.

just some of the factors dealt with at this council. According to Constantine, "Division in the church is worse than war." This ideology of unification of the church shared by Constantine was of more significance than arriving at the truth of this matter, for how could the emperor maintain political control of an empire that was divided with diverse beliefs and dogmas?

In conclusion to the conflict, the perspective of Athanasius was accepted though it lacked any scriptural foundation; it also meant ostracizing a great percentage of the population who accepted the concept of Arius and rejected that of Athanasius.

Various ecumenical councils followed in the coming years to determine what would be identified as Christian doctrine and what would not. After the Council of Nicaea, there was the First Council of Constantinople in 381. At this council, the Nicene Creed was established, seven canons were legislated, four doctrinal and three disciplinary, among other factors designed to establish consensus.

In 431, there was the Council of Ephesus in which the doctrine of Mary being the Mother of God or Theotokos was established. The council denounced the teaching of Bishop Nestorius, who taught that Jesus existed as two persons, the man Jesus and the divine Son of God, or Logos, rather than as a unified person.

British monk Pelagius was also condemned for his teachings, which were opposed to the concept of grace. Pelagius taught that moral perfection was attainable in this life without the assistance of divine grace through human free will. Heresies were condemned, and the council declared it "unlawful for any man to bring forward, or to write, or to compose a different faith as a rival to that established by the holy Fathers assembled with the Holy Ghost in Nicaea."

There were several other councils such as the Council of Chalcedon in 451, the Second Council of Constantinople in 553, the Third Council of Constantinople from 680–681, and finally, the Second Council of Nicaea in 787. The relationship of Jesus and Christ, the Eucharist and concomitance defined as Holy Communion, and the divine maternity dogma of the Blessed Virgin Mary were only a few of the established concepts presently acknowledged as Christian orthodoxy. This is the state instituting the foundation of the church; any teaching, practice, or doctrine not in synch with or in opposition to those established would have been considered heresy and their proponents heretics, a label that meant more than being ostracized; it meant being put to death. The truth may indeed be a bitter pill to swallow but a necessary one if we are to be awakened from our state of slumber and lethargy and become who we were designed to be.

CHAPTER 8

THE BIRTH OF HERESY

> They that approve a private opinion, call it opinion; but they that dislike it, heresy: and yet heresy signifies no more than private opinion.
>
> —Thomas Hobbes (1588–1679), *Leviathan*

Prior to the installation of central authority of the church and the establishment of doctrinal and church orthodoxy, society was free to believe and practice whatever it chose. There were instances of Christian persecution, but such was not necessarily based on doctrinal beliefs. Additionally, there were diverse sects of Christianity that were at loggerheads with each other; of course, the sect with the most authority would attain control and be considered in bed with the state.

These latest developments, however, of the ascribed canon, official policy, set rituals, creeds, and church hierarchy introduced by the state would officially give birth to the notion of heresy, a profane or sacrilegious term given to anyone who believed or taught any doctrine contradictory to what was sanctioned and for which there were grave consequences.

Heresy according to the Online Etymological dictionary is defined as

> doctrine or opinion at variance with established standards" (or, as Johnson defines it, "an opinion

of private men different from that of the catholic and orthodox church"), c. 1200, from Old French heresie, eresie "heresy," and by extension "sodomy, immorality" (12c.), from Latin hæresis, "school of thought, philosophical sect."

The Latin word is from Greek *hairesis,* a taking or choosing for oneself, a choice, a means of taking; a deliberate plan, purpose; philosophical sect, school," from haireisthai "take, seize," middle voice of hairein "to choose," a word of unknown origin, perhaps cognate with Hittite šaru "booty," Welsh herw "booty;" but Beekes offers no etymology.

Besides the various pagan beliefs that were pervasive prior to the inauguration of the ecumenical councils in the third century, Christianity was variegated in a fashion very similar to today. Christianity was not the unified movement as most have been taught to believe. The notion of Christian persecution has been perpetuated by scholars and adherents of the faith for centuries. What isn't outlined, though, is that in most cases, the persecution of Christians was done by other Christians. There were diverse forms of Christian tradition each with its own version of the story of Jesus. The only version that the world would know was the prevailing version of the conquerors. The factor that determined who was the conqueror of course would be based on which sect had the most support.

Some of the diverse Christian sects that existed at the time included these.

The Ebionites

They rose in the first century around the time of the destruction of the Jewish temple in AD 70. The Ebionites included the Nazarenes and the Elkasites; they did not accept the ideology of the virgin birth of Jesus. They proposed the view that Jesus was the son of Joseph and Mary, and they were strict adherents to Jewish law. The Ebionites believed that Jesus became the Messiah because he obeyed Jewish law.

Monarchianism

Perpetuated by Paul of Samosata during the second century, this doctrine held that Jesus was a man who became divine rather than God who became man.

The Marcionites

This sect was named after Marcion and flourished in the second century. The Marcionites claimed that there were two cosmic gods and differentiated the God of the Old Testament from the God of the New Testament. Their ideology proposed that the God of the Old was vengeful and functioned from a position of wrath embodying justice while the God of the New embodied goodness.

Manichaeism

This was a gnostic, dualistic religious movement founded in the third century by Mani, known as the supreme Illuminator and the Apostle of Light. This doctrine purports that one's soul shares in the nature of God but has fallen into the evil world of matter and must be saved by means of the spirit. It claims that to acknowledge one's soul as sharing in the very nature of God is the beginning of self-knowledge.

The Donatists

Derived from their leader, Donatus, this movement lasted from the third to the seventh century. From this movement, other sects were birthed such as the Montanist and the Novatianist movements. The Donatists had differences of doctrinal and social nature and was opposed to state interference in church affairs.

This list is in the least exhaustive. Irenaeus of Lyons, leading representative of Catholic Christianity in the last quarter of the second century and champion of orthodoxy against gnostic[61] heresy, listed at least twenty forms of Christianity that he was aware of. And Epiphanius, bishop of Salamis, another strong defender of orthodoxy, counted no fewer than eighty forms of Christianity at his time.

What is known as Christianity today was never unified or emerged from a singular source. Christianity formed part of a

---

[61] Gnosticism (after *gnôsis*, the Greek word for "knowledge" or "insight") is the name given to a loosely organized religious and philosophical movement that flourished in the first and second centuries AD.

progression in history in which the foundation was pagan. After the involvement of the state via Constantine, the doctrine espoused by Paul, initially rejected by the true followers of Jesus, became the established doctrine, and everything else was identified as heresy.

In the fourth century, the Catholic Church emerged with an agenda to maintain dominance and control, and for the next thousand years, Nicene Christianity wasn't just violent; it was brutal and barbaric doing what it must to totally annihilate the Gnostics, the Marcionites, and any other sect that shared a different belief. This included the destruction and burning of any literature including books and other records.

CHAPTER 9

THE CHRIST CONCEPT

> He whose heart is full of tenderness, and truth;
> Who loves mankind more than he loves himself,
> And cannot find room in his heart to hate, May be another Christ.
>
> —Eric Butterworth

Another factor that continues to evade our understanding is the ideology of Christ. This chapter was intentionally separated from the previous chapter concerning Jesus since even though Jesus and Christ have become synonymous, they are separate entities. This controversial issue continues to baffle theologians and scholars alike; what was the relationship and connection between Jesus and Christ? This incessant argument as to the divinity of a man, about whether he was God manifested in the flesh, whether he was half-man and half-god, or whether he was flesh attaining godship came to a culmination at the Nicaean Council. As also mentioned however, the conclusion arrived at was not necessarily the truth but simply a consensus.

Many people have a totally flawed understanding of the Christ concept. Many are of the view that Christ refers only to Christianity, and so many Christians believe that to accept Christ means to be a Christian. From a religious perspective, that may be so, but as we unearth the history behind the concept, we recognize that Christ is much more than what we have been taught or conditioned to believe and that its reference goes beyond the notion of the man we identify as Jesus. To most, this is the mental picture that automatically arises in reference to the word, and though this impression is seemingly valid, the underlying concept essentially distorts the true essence of the term *Christ*.

Simply put, many people have personified the word *Christ* in the same manner that Jesus is personified. Many believe that Christ is the surname of Jesus, that his full name is Jesus Christ in the same manner your full name might be Sarah McLaughlin, but this is incorrect. The idea of a surname as we do now was nonexistent in biblical times. Persons were identified either by where they resided, their ethnic background, or their ancestry. Jesus for instance was called Jesus of Nazareth, Nazareth being a Jewish town in Galilee, since there have been other persons named Jesus. In similar fashion, Mary of Magdalene hailed from the town Magadala.

In terms of ancestry, there were characters such as Simon bar Jonah (John 1:42), where bar is Aramaic for son; hence, Simon was the son of Jonah. People were also identified according to ethnicity, such as Saul's chief shepherd, Doeg the Edomite (1 Samuel 21:7), who was a descendent of Esau. We know from what is written that Jesus was a normal man of flesh and blood who hungered, thirsted, bled, and felt pain. Whether he was born of a virgin immaculately conceived or conceived via the process of pathogenesis is another issue we dealt with in the previous chapter. What we are desirous of understanding however is his relationship to the title Christ and what that means for us.

Philosophers have argued over the centuries that the Christ concept is nothing more than a human creation born from our need to be saved from our circumstances and ourselves. The ideology insists that there is no historical basis for the existence of Jesus Christ, a concept identified as the Christ myth. This Christ myth is said to have been perpetuated primarily by the self-appointed apostle Paul, who it is claimed had his own agenda that appeared contrary to the agenda of the historical Jesus. Psychologist Karl Jung argued, for example, that when Paul claimed to have met Jesus on the road to Damascus, he was really suffering from a hallucination and that Paul's desire to find a Christ was the true reason he imagined he had that meeting. Even if such was so and Paul's experience was based on his deep-seated desire to know Christ, the same can be said about many people even today.

Many religious people be they Christian, Muslim, Hindu, etc., claim to have had personal experiences with the God they believe in. Though one may have had a personal experience, it is subjective, not objective since one's experiences may simply be a projection of his or her thoughts and beliefs.

Humanists argue that the Christ concept is something found in ourselves, that the proper development of human virtue will eventually lead us to a place where we can reach a higher plane of existence where we will no longer destroy and pervert our or others' lives. Those who believe in God will argue that it is impossible for human beings to set themselves free because of their shortcomings and deficiencies. They argue that our salvation and hope for the future has to come from something or someone outside ourselves. Pantheism[62] argues that nature is the higher power while others postulate that Christ will eventually save us when he returns. What

---

[62] Pantheism is a religious belief that includes the entire universe in its idea of God.

is the truth behind all this philosophical, theological, and intellectual turmoil?

Evaluating the Christ concept is something each person should do personally since such beliefs have a great impact on our society. There are many religions, and most of them claim to be awaiting the appearance or reappearance of a Christ. This means that all of these religions make similar claims to the effect that any member subscribing to their beliefs will eventually be rewarded salvation by a Christlike person, someone anointed and sent personally by God. The question I now ask though is whether the coming of Christ is the same as the coming of a man named Jesus who attained Christhood.

I want you to consider the fruits of each religion that claims to be in possession of the truth concerning the Christ. These beliefs whether at the forefront of our conscious minds or not influence and shape our thoughts about who we are and what we think about ourselves and unconsciously shape our worldviews.

As with the chapter on the God concept, we have seen that all we have accepted without question concerning God is not necessarily so, and soon, the same can be said about the concept of Christ. The word *Christ* is taken from old English Crist, which was taken from the Latin word *Christus* and derived from the Greek word *christos*, meaning to smear or rub with oil or to anoint; Jesus was identified as the Anointed One. It is from this word Christos that the term Christian originates and was used only three times in the Bible.

> And when he had found him, he brought him unto Antioch. And it came to pass, that a whole year they assembled themselves with the church, and

taught much people. And the disciples were called Christians first in Antioch. (Acts 11:26 KJV)

Then Agrippa said unto Paul, Almost thou persuadest me to be a Christian. (Acts 26:28 KJV)

Yet if any man suffer as a Christian, let him not be ashamed; but let him glorify God on this behalf. (1 Peter 4:16 KJV)

This Greek word Christos is a translation of the Hebrew word *Masiah* meaning Messiah, one of Jesus's many titles in the New Testament; however, he was not the only person who was called Messiah as it translates from the word anointed. In Isaiah 45:1, Cyrus was called anointed meaning Messiah: "Thus saith the LORD to his anointed, to Cyrus, whose right hand I have holden, to subdue nations before him; and I will loose the loins of kings, to open before him the two leaved gates; and the gates shall not be shut." Also, in Leviticus 4, it is used a few times in reference to the Levitical priests as well as in 1 Samuel 29:9, where David described Saul: "And David said to Abishai, Destroy him not: for who can stretch forth his hand against the LORD'S anointed, and be guiltless?"

To the Jews, Jesus the Messiah's agenda was primarily political; his mandate according to them was to lead the charge for Jewish liberation. To do this, he would have to be equipped mentally and spiritually and be guided by God in all his actions. This did not make him God in the flesh whether it be God becoming flesh or flesh becoming God. Even before the coming of Jesus, the Jews already had their concept of a Messiah. The ideology of the Gentile Christians was not the same as the Jews'; their philosophy as proposed by Paul and infused by dogma and myth of previous cultures suggested that the Messiah Christ came as a savior to the entire world, that he died and resurrected from the dead, and that he would return for those who accept him.

The notion of being anointed was not only ascribed to Jesus; this however does not eradicate the distinctiveness of his purpose and call. Every human being however also has a specific purpose and mandate while on earth inclusive of their primary responsibility of personal growth and development, and this is so whether people accept it or not.

From research, it was unearthed that anointing someone or something basically meant separating that someone or something from the rest or being set aside by God for a specific purpose. Inanimate things were anointed such as the tabernacle in Exodus 40:9, the altar in Exodus 29:36, and the tent and the ark in Exodus 30:26 to name a few.

Scripturally, many were anointed for specific purposes such as Aaron and his sons in Numbers 3:2–3 and various other references in Exodus and Leviticus. We saw kings being anointed such as David, who was anointed on three occasions with each instance being based on an agenda; in 1 Samuel 16:13, David was anointed king of Israel; in 2 Samuel 2:4, the men of Judah anointed David to be king of Judah; and in 2 Samuel 5:3, David was anointed king of Israel. These anointings were performed by men. In Leviticus 8:30, Moses anointed Aaron; in 1 Samuel 9:16, Samuel anointed Saul; in 11 Samuel 2:7, the men of Judah anointed David; in 1 Samuel 12:20, David anointed himself; and in 1 Kings 1:34, Zadok and Nathan anointed Solomon.

This was not the case with Jesus. Further, in several versions of the Bible, the word *anointed* was lowercased for all but Jesus, for which the word was uppercased. Some versions differentiate between "an anointed one" and "the Anointed One" in reference to Jesus.

Let's examine the anointing as it relates to Jesus. In Luke 4:14, Jesus stated,

> The Spirit of the Lord is upon me, because he hath anointed me to preach the gospel to the poor; he hath sent me to heal the brokenhearted, to preach deliverance to the captives, and recovering of sight to the blind, to set at liberty them that are bruised.

Jesus claimed to have been anointed by the Spirit of the Lord. This sentiment is reiterated in Acts 10:38: "How God anointed Jesus of Nazareth with the Holy Ghost and with power: who went about doing good, and healing all that were oppressed of the devil; for God was with him." Numerous scriptures mention God anointing Jesus, but when did this anointing occur? Was it at the time of Jesus's baptism at the Jordan by John the Baptist?

This is according to Luke 3:21–21.

> Now when all the people were baptized, Jesus was also baptized, and while He was praying, heaven was opened, and the Holy Spirit descended upon Him in bodily form like a dove, and a voice came out of heaven, "You are My beloved Son, in You I am well-pleased."

And Matthew 3:16–17 tells us,

> After being baptized, Jesus came up immediately from the water; and behold, the heavens were opened, and he saw the Spirit of God descending as a dove and lighting on Him, and behold, a voice out of the heavens said, "This is My beloved Son, in whom I am well-pleased."

God anointed Jesus personally making the occasion distinct and intimate. This occurrence in itself separates the act of anointing persons throughout history and the scripture from that of Jesus.

In Colossians 1:2, the apostle Paul stated, "To them God has chosen to make known among the Gentiles the glorious riches of this mystery, which is Christ in you, the hope of glory." Paul was stating that Christ dwelled in us, a novel concept. However, because we have been conditioned to accept Christ as the man who walked the earth some two thousand years ago, we erroneously attempt to assimilate this perspective in our metal schema, which like so many other perspectives cannot fit. Additionally, it is also written in John 1:5, "The light shineth in darkness; and the darkness comprehended it not." John 1 was explored in the previous chapter whereby an attempt was made to include Jesus in the beginning by personification of the word *word* and exchanging the word *it* for the word *him*.

This word spoken about in John 1:1 was indeed the essence of God; this wasn't Jesus though as taught but the Christ. From this, one can infer that Christ exists in all people despite their religion, ethnicity, or culture. According to Rupert Furneaux in *The Other Side of The Story*,

> The Jewish term "Messiah" and the Christian word "Christ" are two totally different conceptions. While both mean "Anointed One," to the Jews the Messiah was a Savior King who would free his people from bondage. To the Gentile Christian the term "Christ" meant a World Redeemer, the legendary dying and rising god, who would save mankind from the bondage of original sin.[63]

The Jews and the Gentile Christians then did not grasp the essence of the Christ whom Jesus introduced to humanity.

Having Christ in our beings is like having any body part like a kidney or a heart, and one's failure to accept or acknowledge that reality does not make it any different. That light spoken about that dwells in the darkness according to John 1:5 is none other than the Christ principle. Although Jesus was a human being like all people, most of us are ignorant of what it truly means to fully be a human being.

The way that the human being is designed is still beyond what the highest level of natural science has described or understands. We are multidimensional (existing on various dimensions simultaneously) and electromagnetic (dealing with electrical and magnetic fields); we are energetic and spiritual. Our physical bodies including all our major organs and systems are simply the gross manifestation of what we are. Deficiencies in our higher state would eventually manifest in this dense form as ice is a dense form of water. All physical ailments

---

[63] Furneaux, Rupert. "The Other Side of The Story." (Cassell & Company, London, 1953).

and diseases have at their core some deficiency or imbalance in our higher states.

Our core, our soul, is an intangible component still unexplored by science and basically unknown. Having a full grasp and understanding of this aspect of our being is the beginning of our humanness. The notion of simply identifying Jesus or any man for that matter without taking all these factors into consideration is critical.

Indeed, Jesus was a man but a vastly conscious and exceedingly evolved man who understood all aspects of his being. The soul ascribed to Jesus in this earth plane would have been a highly evolved and very mature soul. He would have understood his purpose and knew that he knew; he would have been conscious of his consciousness. He was not subject to the state of amnesia we all experience on our physical manifestation in this three-dimensional reality. Now take this highly evolved man and activate the Christ potential within him and what will you get? A man who can declare with authority according to Philippians 4:13, "I can do all things through Christ which strengthened me." This scripture was no cliché to Jesus, and he was not afraid of equating himself with the father; hence, his utterances of him and the father being one notwithstanding he was not the father, but the very essence of the father within him was activated and expressed. Jesus became in totality a conduit for Christ to the point that there was no distinction between him and the Christ, hence attaining the title Jesus the Christ.

This was the conflict that existed between Arius and Athanasius. Arius recognized that Jesus was a man, and Athanasius thought it blasphemous to think so recognizing that the power with which Jesus functioned was beyond that of flesh and blood. What both men failed to recognize at that time was the dynamics of the human being, the notion of DNA, epigenetics,[64] the soul and state of consciousness. They failed to realize that the ways we are designed are far more than what meets the eye. This was the mandate and purpose of Jesus on earth, but he was highly evolved, and the activation and expression of the Christ potential within him, which he allowed at most times to guide all aspects of his life, made him God in the flesh.

This display was indeed beyond anything ever known to humanity at that time since humanity was not as insightful as we are now; we have consciously progressed exponentially over the years. Jesus was a way-shower, a model, an example; his mandate was to educate, empower, and perpetuate a total paradigm shift in the hearts and minds of people duplicating himself. Jesus's agenda meant recruiting disciples, a term given not just to followers but to those who were disciplined since we all possess the ability to epitomize the Christ principle but such requires discipline.

Jesus recognized that most of society wasn't consciously ready for what he had to give, though, and this was expressed in John 16:12 when he told his disciples, "I have yet many things to say unto you, but ye cannot bear them now." This view was further elaborated by the apostle Paul in 1 Corinthians 3:2, when he said, "I have fed you with milk, and not with meat: for hitherto ye were not able to bear it, neither yet now are ye able." I want to stress on the word *consciously* when I wrote that "society wasn't consciously ready" since one may perceive that Jesus came before his time.

---

[64] Epigenetics literally means above or on top of genetics. It refers to external modifications to DNA that turn genes on or off. These modifications do not change the DNA sequence but affect how cells "read" genes.

Nothing happens randomly in the universe, and there are no mistakes even though things may not go the way we desire them to go. Jesus's mere presence was sufficient to shift the vibrational frequency of the planet and activate the Christ potential in many. From a cognitive perspective, the mental state of the population may not have been on the vibratory frequency to receive what Jesus could have given; however, on a subconscious level, lives were being impacted and transformation was taking place. Jesus never sought to speak or elaborate on higher mysteries to the general population but taught via simplistic metaphors and parables, values of living, harmony, peace, and love most of which were related to agrarian principles being synonymous with the era of the time.

The ideology of shedding his blood to save humanity has been accepted by many, but an understanding of this process was never outlined. How does the execution of a man and the shedding of his blood affect all others? The essence of the agenda and mandate of Jesus was being fulfilled below the conscious threshold of humanity.

Today, science has advanced beyond the notion of matter and particles to quantum dynamics; that allows us to get a better although not complete understanding of a process that would have had no real significance to people at the time of this occurrence. Scientists are only now realizing that the notion of time being linear—past, present, and future—is perhaps illusionary. Jesus's shedding his blood is highly significant. Most of us can verbalize what we believe, but because we lack understanding of what we believe, most of what we say are clichés based primarily on what we have learned.

Let's establish some degree of meaning and make sense of where this blood is concerned. Blood has always been acknowledged as something very powerful naturally; it is known that life itself is in the blood. We can also notice that any deeply significant event involves some degree of blood flow such as the rupturing of a female's hymen the first time upon having sex or the process of giving birth. There are also circumstances where persons make blood bonds, where agreements or contracts are sealed with blood. Throughout the Old Testament are numerous instances involving blood sacrifices for consecration or purification. Blood intensifies any agenda since there is a component to it that is unseen to the naked eye.

Jesus's blood was highly potent, especially after it became infused with the Christ principle. Spilling this blood had serious consequences beyond time and space. Upon being released in the atmosphere, the essence of that blood started reverberating and has not stopped. Everything vibrates and radiates at a specific frequency; that means that all who choose to believe in their hearts and minds become synchronized with the frequency activating the Christ potential, which exists in all people. This process occurs below the threshold of our consciousness. By having an understanding of the energetic, a term that the religious minded may identify as the spiritual, the shedding of his blood touching all lives became possible.

The effect of the releasing of the blood of Jesus in the atmosphere can be compared to the releasing of nuclear energy as was done when atomic bombs were dropped in Hiroshima and Nagasaki in 1945 but with a greater potency and effect albeit in a positive and uplifting way. Researchers have identified that the effects of this nuclear disaster in 1945 continued in various ways for over seventy years. A new component was released in the earth's atmosphere with Jesus's execution, a component that is available to all people once they can elevate their vibrational frequency and allow for a vibrational match.

The notion of a man identified as Christ bursting through the clouds on a chariot to save humanity is preposterous. The notion of dead people being raised from the grave for judgment at his coming is even more absurd. I guess the practice of cremation and scattering one's burnt remains in the ocean was nonexistent at the time of this concept. Christ is a potential principle that exists in each one of us; failure to connect with this principle spells failure to function fully in the way we were designed. We can and will come alive or be awakened from the dead state in which we exist only when this connection is made; Christ will then return and indeed the dead in Christ will arise.

CHAPTER 10

THE CONCEPT OF DEATH

> I do not fear death. I had been dead for billions and billions of years before I was born, and had not suffered the slightest inconvenience from it.
>
> —Mark Twain

Just the thought of death is taboo though we know that it is the one conclusion we will all face. Why does a subconscious sense of fear engulf us when the subject of death arises? Most of our fears are usually the result of our ignorance of whatever we fear. Death represents an unknown end, a conclusion; few of us desire to get there since it appears to be in opposition to life.

But death is not the opposite of life; life includes death, and death is a part of life. They do not oppose each other. Further, there is no such thing as dead matter; life is one, and it cannot be changed except into itself. All forms are forms of this unity and must come and go through some inner activity. This inner activity of life or nature must be some form of self-consciousness or self-knowing. In our human understanding, we would call this inner knowing or conscious thought.

There is always life even in death; what occurs in death is a transition, not a conclusion. A wonderful analogy is the death of a caterpillar leading to the birth of a butterfly. However, not all transitions occur this way; our physical reality is only the gross manifestation of its etheric essence. Water is the gross physical reality of two hydrogen atoms with one oxygen atom that vibrates at a particular rate but cannot be observed with the naked eye.

Human beings go through various transitions in life physical and otherwise most of which are not observable or detected by the five senses. In the womb, a unicellular organism becomes multicellular and a full-grown fetus by nine months, and then it enters a new life in the world in which it goes through more life-changing processes. These changes are physical, psychological, emotional, and spiritual. His or her final transition in physical reality occurs when he or she sheds the physical body, becomes detached from societal identity, and continues to exist in another vibratory plane of existence determined by that soul's personal vibratory state and consciousness. There is a spiritual death and a physical death, and it is not necessary to die physically in order to die spiritually.

Spiritual Death

Spiritual death is a person's separation from God, from his or her source, supply, or essence. Humans are souls living in bodies and energized by spirit and not merely the body itself. The human body is a mere shell, an electromagnetic, biogenetic case that houses the essence of a person but is totally infused with the person's etheric essence; hence, deficiencies in the energetic manifest as diseases in the physical body. As a result, the essence of a person cannot die, just his or her temporal form of three-dimensional existence and identity.

The life force or essence of humans is from God, and this essence is eternal as God is. If God were the ocean, humans could be identified as the waves. Both are distinct, but one is the result of the other. All people are spiritually dead until they awaken to their spiritual selves and regain God consciousness; not all people accomplish this in one lifetime. (The dead in Christ shall rise.)

What was responsible for this state of death all people were born into? It is proposed that death came as a result of what is called sin. Please note that the concept of sin is erroneous. Sin is not an act but a state of mind, a state of delusion, and belief in an illusion. According to Hindu philosophy, such a state is called Maya. The word *sin* was derived from the Hebrew word *Khata* and the Greek word *Harmartia*, which mean to fail or to miss the mark. What mark does humanity miss? This unidentified mark has been abused by the religious minded for centuries since it allows for anyone to infer anything to castigate and lay blame as in the case of heresy.

According to Isaiah 59:2, sin separates humans from God: "But your iniquities have separated between you and your God, and your sins have hid his face from you, that he will not hear." Sin lowers our vibrational state, which prevents us from resonating on our highest frequency and hinders and separates us from connecting within to God. It reasons that once we fail to identify and connect with the Christ within, all our actions would in some way fail and can be identified as sinful. Any thought that perpetuates separation, that fails to take into account the oneness of all things, and that is based on an agenda of personal gain at the expense of others is derived from a place of sin. It means that any action taken from such position would miss the mark.

All humanity is born in this state; Romans 5:12 reads, "Wherefore, as by one man sin entered into the world, and death by sin; and so death passed upon all men, for that all have sinned." The sociology of one generation affected all future generations. These acts led to degeneration, devolution—the fall of humankind. It means we are all born dead or inert to our true essence, the activation of which requires conscious effort and discipline.

Once we are in a state of sin, all our actions, which are falsely identified as sin, would not correspond to the welfare and well-being of the universal whole and would always fall short of the divine essence. According to Romans 3:23, "For all have sinned, and come short of the glory of God."

The first death was a separation from God. When Adam sinned, he lost touch with his divinity. He hid himself because he lost spiritual consciousness and gained earthly consciousness (Genesis 3:7–10). He discovered he was naked; prior to that, he was spiritually minded and fellowshipped with God in the cool of the day. (Please note that this story in Genesis is an allegory and should not be taken literally.)

Death is separation from the God life, our true essence; that is why it takes the renewing of our mind and connecting with Christ within to establish a link back to our divinity. Christ is our link to our God life, our real life. There can be no true life without reconnecting to that essence. Life outside of Christ is spiritual death. Death began with humankind's noncompliance with the directive and will of their divine essence.

The Bible Account of Sin as the Original Cause of Death

God commanded Adam not to eat from the Tree of the Knowledge of Good and Evil and warned, "For in the day you eat from it, you shall surely die" (Genesis 2:17). It is at this juncture that man experienced the first death and transitioned from consciousness of our connectedness with God and lost a connection with the source of life. Adam and Eve began to live in the flesh and lose touch with the life-giving Spirit. They began to reverse the flow of the life force, the élan vital,[65] bringing it further into self-consciousness. This became so acute that we actually experienced a death of the spirit; we died to the spiritual influence.

Adam, Eve, and the serpent (all aspects of ourselves) fell from grace and lost the comfort of the garden. The Tree of Life, symbolizing immortality, is now protected from us so we don't become eternally terrestrial beings when we are eternally celestial beings. Now we enter the cycle of life and death as we know it today.

This is further symbolized metaphysically in Eve's conception of Cain and Abel. Cain means the acquired one (our forming egos), and Abel means a breath or soul, our spiritually aware selves (Genesis 4). God favors the offerings of our souls more than our egos as symbolized in Abel's offering as opposed to Cain's, prompting Cain (ego) to kill Abel (soul). The Lord told Cain,

> Why are you angry, and why has your countenance fallen? If you do well, will you not be accepted? And if you do not do well, sin is couching at the door [of your consciousness]; its desire is for you, but you must master it. (Genesis 4:6–7)

This is the great call to us. Self-consciousness if driven by the ego can lead to self-centeredness and loss of union with the whole.

---

[65] *Élan vital* is the vital force or impulse of life, a creative principle held by French philosopher Henri Bergson in his 1907 book *Creative Evolution*, to be immanent in all organisms and responsible for evolution.

We simply must as the Lord God said in the garden, "Subdue the earth [i.e., our self-centered urges]" (Genesis 1:28). And as the Lord said to our Cain selves, "You must master it [self-will]." By gaining control over this powerful gift, we will come to know ourselves to be ourselves and yet become one with the whole.

We died to the spirit and gave birth to the self. The spirit and the universal consciousness of God is the true source and nature of life, so when we died to it, we lost immortality and wisdom. And since God is spirit, we also lost consciousness of God. This is symbolized by our being denied access to the Tree of Life (Genesis 3:22–24). If we partook of the Tree of Life in the state we were in, we would have condemned ourselves to a state of Maya. We also began to develop an even stronger sense of self to the point that we lost awareness of self's connectedness to the whole—God and other souls.

This mounting sense of self and development of the ego perpetuates the illusion of the separation of I versus you and we versus them and obscures the truth that everything is all connected in a deep and profound way. It is for this reason that Jesus, when asked what was the greatest commandment in Matthew 22:36–40, responded as he did.

> Master, which is the great commandment in the law? Jesus said unto him, Thou shalt love the Lord thy God with all thy heart, and with all thy soul, and with all thy mind. This is the first and great commandment. And the second is like unto it, Thou shalt love thy neighbor as thyself. On these two commandments hang all the law and the prophets.

These first two commandments supersede all law because once one becomes one with God and sees no separation between oneself and another, which is in essence the truth of all existence, life takes on a whole new meaning. The veil of Maya, the illusion of reality, lifts and life takes on a new meaning. The question was put to Indian sage Ramana Maharshi, "How should we treat others?" His response was, "There are no others." The response of Maharshi is reflective of a transcendent soul. He saw beyond the illusion identified by the ego mind and the state of sin.

To regain God consciousness, this movement from the spirit to the self must be turned around. Jesus said to Nicodemus, "Unless one is born anew, he cannot see the kingdom of God … That which is born of the flesh is flesh, and that which is born of the Spirit is spirit" (John 3:3, 6). We have been born of flesh, which makes us sons and daughters of humans, but we must also be born of the Spirit, which makes us sons and daughters of God. During our physical lives, we should strive to experience the second birth, the birth of the spirit. This is spoken of and symbolized many times in the Bible as well as the Quran and other holy texts.

We must yield to the will of the spirit in us and allow it to have expression in our lives. If we seek its way more than our own, it will eventually be fully manifest. We will be once again spiritual beings in the physical world. As Jesus stated, "When you have lifted up the son of man, then you will know." (John 8:28). When we have raised our earthly selves to the level of consciousness of our heavenly selves, we will know what it's all about and who we really are.

Physical Death

Physical death is the withdrawal of earthly consciousness. Our fear of death makes us miss the truth that death in terms of annihilation is impossible. This physical life is simply a temporary expression of the eternal transcendental energy and consciousness that is us. There is no death, and therefore, there can be no loss. People are spiritual beings like God, and spirits cannot die. Here is what King Solomon who as recorded in the Bible was the wisest man of all time said about death in Ecclesiastes 12:5–8.

> Also when they shall be afraid of that which is high, and fears shall be in the way, and the almond tree shall flourish, and the grasshopper shall be a burden, and desire shall fail: because man goes to his long home, and the mourners go about the streets: Or ever the silver cord be loosed, or the golden bowl be broken, or the pitcher be broken at the fountain, or the wheel broken at the cistern. Then shall the dust return to the earth as it was: and the spirit shall return to God who gave it. Vanity of vanities, said the preacher; all is vanity.

The body returns to the earth and the spirit return to God. Humans cannot die; they are released from their earthly confinements and societal identities and return home. We are here to grow, to expand, and to evolve, which occurs via the many lessons life brings us or from those we attract. Expansion and evolution include liberation, detachment, forgiveness, balance, releasing of negative karma, etc. Earth is a school of learning; all our experiences good, bad, or indifferent are designed to expand us. The faster we learn the lesson, which is love, the faster we move along. Becoming older in terms of physical years and possibly dying in whatever way is not an indicator of being spiritually evolved just as chronological age is not an indicator of maturational age.

Many of our contemporary leaders including those in the clergy identify the development and expression of our gifts and talents as the purpose of our existence on earth. This is a truth but not the total truth or the core truth, and in many instances, it can be very misleading. We are all born with a significant purpose, but the notions of fame, money, and stature attributed to the fulfillment of such purposes are all worldly illusions designed for entrapment and egoistic ideals.

When Jesus was asked why a blind man he had healed had been born that way, Jesus replied, "Neither this man nor his parents sinned ... but this happened so that the works of God might be displayed in him." We read in Romans 9:17, "For the scripture saith unto Pharaoh, Even for this same purpose have I raised thee up, that I might shew my power in thee, and that my name might be declared throughout all the earth." In spite of our earthly purpose, our ultimate agenda is to evolve and to know the truth about what we are, which in itself serves the greater good of humanity. According to Maharshi, "Your own Self-realization is the greatest service you can render the world." This is further echoed in the poem "Invictus" by Marriane Williamson made popular by Nelson Mandela: "As we are liberated from our fears our presence automatically liberates others."

According to 1 Corinthians 15:54–56,

> But when this perishable will have put on the imperishable, and this mortal will have put on

immortality, then will come about the saying that is written, "death is swallowed up in victory. O death, where is your victory? o death, where is your sting The sting of death is sin, and the power of sin is the law; But thanks be to God! He gives us the victory through our Lord Jesus Christ.

Our victory over death is in Christ, who releases in us the power of immortality. To acknowledge Christ is to acknowledge a potential principle in us. We should acknowledge this potential principle, develop it, become one with it, see the world through the lens of it, and watch the perishable become imperishable and the mortal become immortal.

CHAPTER 11

LIFE AFTER DEATH

Death is not extinguishing the light; it is only putting out the lamp because the dawn has come.

—Rabindranath Tagore

The first law of thermodynamics, the law of conservation of energy, states that energy can neither be created nor destroyed but only changed from one form to another. As indicated in a previous chapter, human beings are electromagnetic by nature. To the religious who may not grasp or embrace science, being electromagnetic is synonymous with being spiritual as is often stated in church as, "We are spiritual beings having a physical experience." Scientific laws as they pertains to energy (spirit) are applicable to us because by our very nature we are energetic. We are spiritual/energetic beings encased in physical bodies.

As I mentioned, death is not an end but a transition. This topic may be highly controversial specifically in the Christian fraternity, but we need to understand it if we are to ever come to a more comprehensive understanding of life itself, its meaning, and our purpose. A holistic understanding of spiritual matters would remain a permanent mystery to those who refuse to accept this concept. Some think that such ideology is flawed and fictitious. They believe the concept of life after death is so vague that we should be more concerned with this life. If, however, the position is taken that all life is one flow that simply transitions, having an understanding of life beyond physical life may guide us in this life and give much more meaning to it.

There is no afterlife, just a continuity of life, and knowing this should cause us to strive to live our best lives whether in this current form or another. Just as what a caterpillar does consciously or subconsciously in that stage of its existence affects its future state as a butterfly, our actions yield consequences beyond our physical states.

If energy cannot be created or destroyed but only transformed, our essence cannot be destroyed. Our bodies die and decay; they return to elements of nature or the wheel of life as described in some cultures. Ashes to ashes and dust to dust, but that concept highlights our physical aspects, not our essence. What happens to that?

Human beings are energetic by nature, an aspect that simply transforms, but upon death, does the consciousness of this being remain intact? What aspects of our consciousness continue if it does at all? The scientific/psychological and the religious/spiritual domains have thoughts on that.

To the materialists, death signifies an end, a conclusion; we cease to exist in any form after death. Some religious bodies propose that human beings have only one life to live after which they go to heaven or hell based on the lives they led prior to death, a transition.

Some religious sects believe that upon death, the energetic essence or the soul is unaware of anything but will be awakened or resurrected on Judgment Day, receive new physical bodies, stand before the throne of God, and be judged for their deeds while alive.

The Roman Catholic Church also includes the concept of purgatory. According to Merriam-Webster, purgatory is "an intermediate state after death for expiatory purification specifically;

a place or state of punishment wherein the souls of those who die in God's grace may make satisfaction for past sins and so become fit for heaven." It is a place for the souls that may have fallen short to make amends prior to going to heaven. These are just a few of the ideologies concerning life after death.

Only materialists and some atheists proclaim that death is an end to it all. All other ideologies share the commonality of some form of continuity of life after physical death whether it is that of resurrection or reincarnation. The philosophy of the Druids espoused similar afterlife variables including transmigration of the soul, continuity of earthly obligations, and spirits finding abode in places, animals, and even objects. In similar fashion to purgatory, a place called Summerland is identified where souls reside temporarily before embodying another human body.

The ideologies of the Native Americans vary on the concept of life after death. To some, the souls of the departed reside in the spirit world but may communicate via dreams with persons in the physical realm. In other tribes, there is no afterworld since the departed souls are reincarnated as newborns in their clans. Others believe the souls of the deceased become stars or part of the earth.

In ancient Egyptian culture, human beings possessed a Ka (life force) and a Ba (spirit). They believed that death or transition was only a temporary interruption in life and that life continued in the afterlife after a journey. The Egyptians mummified the dead believing the dead would need their bodies in the afterlife. In Shamanism, there is no death; its adherents believe that the soul lives forever and simply goes through various regeneration processes. Others believe that the reality after death is determined by our beliefs; thus our personal convictions as well as the collective consciousness of the society would dictate the course and experience of the soul after death.

Resurrection is the coming of life again in the same being while reincarnation involves a soul taking on a different body, animal, plant, or thing. The concept of reincarnation has many facets. I am inclined to concur with the ideology of reincarnation based primarily on the first law of thermodynamics, but an understanding of the actual process is still not conclusive to me. Let's briefly examine this concept.

Reincarnation is a major tenet of primarily Indian religions such as Jainism, Hinduism, Buddhism, and Sikhism. Its ideologies can be found in Hindu texts such as the Vedas, the Upanishads (Puranas) and the Bhagavad Gita. Yajurveda 4.15 states,

> Whenever we take birth, may our deeds be such that we get a pure mind, long life, good health, vitality, intellect, strong sense organs and a powerful body. In next life also, keep us away from bad deeds and indulge us in noble actions.

In the Gita, Krishna is quoted as saying, "Just as a man discards worn out clothes and puts on new clothes, the soul discards worn out bodies and wear new ones." (2:22). The philosophy of reincarnation is intertwined with the law of karma from which comes karmic debt and karmic lessons. According to Wikipedia, karma means

> action, work or deed; it also refers to the spiritual principle of cause and effect where intent and actions of an individual (cause) influences the future of that individual (effect). Good intent and good deeds

contribute to good karma and future happiness while bad intent and bad deeds contribute to bad karma and future suffering.

This is but a summary of the concept of karma, considered a universal law in Hinduism and Buddhism, and it functions with mathematical precision; reincarnation is very significant in those religions.

Some say the notion of karma is synonymous within the biblical context of sowing and reaping, cause and effect, as cited in numerous scriptures such as Galatians 6:7: "Do not be deceived: God is not mocked, for whatever one sows, that will he also reap," and Job 4:8: "As I have seen, those who plow iniquity and sow trouble reap the same." According to Christian doctrine though, re-embodiment or reincarnation is not the mechanism through which such a law is enacted. The movement of life in this doctrine is espoused to be linear, and as such, the cyclical nature of reincarnation is not applicable since there is no return after death, only judgment.

The philosophy of reincarnation states that upon death, the soul and subtle body go to a different plane or sphere of existence or Loka (Sanskrit), of which there are many divided into higher and lower spheres. Each Loka vibrates at a different frequency but has the same spatial existence. The primary objective of reincarnation is for the soul to transcend lower physical desires until it becomes liberated from them and becomes one with the supreme self in a state called Moksha. This process involves the soul going through numerous births and deaths in the earth realm, where lower physical desires and attachments are released in a process identified as a universal law called Samsara.

Although this concept was not endorsed in Western philosophies and particularly Christianity, various sects shared the concept during the early church period. The historical and sociological context at that time should be noted (see previous chapter). It is proposed that Christian theologians such as gnostic theologian Valentinus (100–160) and Basilides of Alexandria, an early Christian gnostic religious teacher in Alexandria, Egypt, who taught from 117 to 138, taught the doctrine of reincarnation. Early church father Origen, who taught on the preexistence of souls, was also touted as having accepted the doctrine of reincarnation; this however was not confirmed as diverse scholars shared opposing views pertaining to the stance of Origen, views of course based on their subjective inclinations.

Numerous scriptures allude to reincarnation such as Matthew 11:14, where Jesus supposedly connected John the Baptist with Elijah: "And if you are willing to accept it, John himself is Elijah who was to come." This is further endorsed in Mark 9:11–13.

> And they asked him, saying, Why say the scribes that Elias must first come? And he answered and told them, Elias verily cometh first, and restoreth all things; and how it is written of the Son of man, that he must suffer many things, and be set at nought. But I say unto you, that Elias is indeed come, and they have done unto him whatsoever they listed, as it is written of him.

Also Revelation 3:12: "To him who overcomes I will make a pillar in the temple of my God. Never again will he leave it." This implies that those who overcome lower desires and attachment would not be caught in the cyclic nature of reincarnation having to not leave

Moksha: "Never again will he leave it." Malachi 1 tells us that God loved Jacob before he was born. How could God love someone before he was born unless of course he existed before birth? This of course can be interpreted in diverse ways based on one's beliefs.

In Matthew 24:30–34, Jesus said, "Truly I tell you, this generation will certainly not pass away until all these things have happened." Was the generation mentioned here in reference to a definite time span or a specific cultural context? Generational length is ordinarily accepted as being the number of years between the birth of a parent and a child. Abraham was eighty-six when he had Ishmael and a hundred when he had Isaac; hence, the average generational length would be ninety-three years. This figure would vary considerably as a result of social conditions, biological states, environmental factors, and so on. The same can be said if we were to identify or define its meaning in the framework of our culture.

At the core of national cultural differences are values that are learned in the formative years of a child and as such are deep seated and may take generations to change. With this in mind, the ideology being proposed by Jesus that this generation would not pass away is very ambiguous; any attempt to identify a set time frame is near impossible. If we were to use figures as proposed by the authorities, a generational length could span between fifteen to thirty-five years; according to biblical experts however, a biblical generation is no more than forty years.

If we were to use the greater figure of forty years to constitute a generation, how was it possible for Jesus, who existed over two thousand years ago, to say that the generation he was speaking to would not have passed away until all these things he had identified had occurred?

Similar sentiments are in Matthew 16:28: "Verily I say unto you, There be some standing here, which shall not taste of death, till they see the Son of man coming in his kingdom," and Luke 9:27: "But I tell you of a truth, there be some standing here, which shall not taste of death, till they see the kingdom of God." If Jesus had been telling the truth, how do we justify these scriptures?

Many interpretations and ideologies are proposed by religious authorities in a bid to validate and rationalize what Jesus meant by this statement since clearly all the disciples and their generation have passed away. Some has inferred that he was speaking about his resurrection or Pentecost; others stated that he was referring to his transfiguration on the mount. In both instances, however, the time would have been too short to connect it with persons passing away. Others believe that he meant his second coming and the end of history, while some indicate that he was not referring to his actual self but to the coming of the Holy Spirit at Pentecost. The reincarnationists also offer a perspective on this quagmire using the concept of reincarnation as a possible explanation.

Numerous other scriptural references are alluded to to validate reincarnation such as John 9:1.

> And as he was passing by, he saw a man blind from birth. And his disciples asked him, "Rabbi, who has sinned, this man or his parents, that he should be born blind?" Jesus answered, "Neither has this man sinned, nor his parents, but the works of God were to be made manifest in him."

The question posed by the disciples alludes to the state of the man being blind as a result of sin, but he had been blind since birth.

Could it be that his sin occurred in vitro or before his birth? This in itself gives credence to existence prior to manifestation and the possibility of reincarnation.

Even Jesus posed a question to the disciples to which their response alluded to reincarnation being real when he asked his disciples in Mark 8:27, "Whom do people say that I am?" Their responses identified him with John the Baptist, Elijah, or one of the Old Testament prophets. Why would the disciples make such a suggestion, which was not met with any sort of inhibition or correction from Jesus, unless of course reincarnation was indeed an accepted concept at that time?

Numbers 14:18 states, "The Lord is slow to anger, abounding in love and forgiving sin and rebellion. Yet he does not leave the guilty unpunished; he punishes the children for the sin of the parents to the third and fourth generation," while Deuteronomy 5:9 reads,

> You shall not bow down to them or worship them; for I, the Lord your God, am a jealous God, punishing the children for the sin of the parents to the third and fourth generation of those who hate me, [translated, "visiting the iniquity of fathers on children, and on the third and on the fourth 'generation' of those that hate me"].

When we understand universal laws such as the law of attraction, the law of reciprocity and karma, etc., we will recognize that no one can be held responsible for the sins of another. It's like stating that I should be placed in detention in school because my father who attended the school forty years before I did had not submitted some homework. Even Jesus stated that each person should carry his or her own cross in Luke 14:27, while Paul uttered in Galatians 6:5 that every person should bear his or her own burden. Why would a just God punish future generations for the sins of their parents?

I know that many blame our present state of ignorance on Adam and Eve sinning or blame our present societal decay and decadence on the actions of those who have gone before us. The law of cause and effect must be understood. If one generation is destroying the ozone layer, the forests, or the ecosystem, the generations that follow will be negatively affected, but can this be regarded as synonymous with what is outlined in Luke 14:27 and Galatians 6:5?

Let us analyze and dissect these scriptures with a view of unearthing what they truly mean. The Hebrew translation for the word *generation* is *dowr*, a revolution of time; it also means dwelling. Our human body is depicted in the Bible as a temporal dwelling; therefore, this scripture could be interpreted in this manner: "… on the third and fourth reincarnation [bodily dwelling] of those who hate me."

The concept of preexistence and reincarnation is purported to have been declared heresy at the second council of Constantinople in 553, where early church father Origen of Alexandria, also known as Origen Adamantius, appears to have played a critical role in this hypothesis. Origen was noted as one of the most important theologians and biblical scholars of the early Greek Church after the apostles. Some of his work included the extensive *Hexapla*, On the Resurrection (*Peri anastaseos*), Miscellanies (*Stromateis*), and On First Principles. In what may be described as a paradox, Origen has been hailed as both the father of orthodoxy and the father of heresy since he contributed greatly to the development of the church foundation before he was excommunicated after his death and declared a heretic for some of his views. It is alleged that one of the reasons he was anathematized had to do with his ideology on preexistence and reincarnation.

There is an incessant debate among many contemporary theologians, Gnostics, and other authorities concerning what Origen truly believed and advocated. To the theologians, his work did not include any beliefs about reincarnation as it is identified by those who accept it today. To them, his ideology on preexistence was not the same as reincarnation.

According to the advocates of reincarnation, there are three main reasons a soul would reincarnate—it has lessons to learn, it is necessary to evolve to the fullness of its divine nature and become one with God, or its needs to work out karmic debts. Those against the concept claim that reincarnation tends to diminish the Christian concept of salvation. They indicate that no one alive has any recollection of their past lives. This suggestion has been challenged by many including American psychiatrist, hypnotherapist, and author Brian Leslie Weiss, Dr. Ian Stevenson, and Dr. Michael Newton, founder of the Newton Institute. Dr. Newton held a doctorate in counseling psychology, was a certified master hypnotherapist, a member of the American Counseling Association, and wrote several books. Dr. Newton was a former atheist who accepted the ideology of the existence of a God only after having personal experiences of life after death and reincarnation via his hypnotherapy practice. Dr. Stevenson however never relied on hypnotherapy to verify that an individual had a previous life; instead, he chose to research and amass thousands of cases involving children who spontaneously (without hypnosis) remembered past lives.

Further arguments against the concept of reincarnation indicate that it opposes the ideology of the resurrection of the physical body on the Day of Judgment. Although impossibility is a fallacy, especially as it pertains to matters of the etheric and the spiritual, it is beyond mind-boggling to consider that every person dead would arise from the grave and take up a physical body again. Adherents of the orthodox suggest that scriptures utilized by reincarnationists to validate their ideology are all speculative and as such should not be accepted.

The primary verse of scripture utilized by theologians and Christian authorities to invalidate the concept of reincarnation is Hebrews 9:27: "And as it is appointed unto men once to die, but after this the judgment." Unfortunately (as with a number of other verses in the Bible), our overreliance on the perceived literalization and perfection of our translations may tend to obscure the true meaning of this verse since further examination of this scripture can also be interpreted in the following manner: "Everyone dies, and after this comes a debriefing [a life review in order to plan the next one]."

CHAPTER 12

HEAVEN AND HELL

> I don't like to commit myself about heaven and hell—you see, I have friends in both places.
>
> —Mark Twain

Another critical concept deep in the psyche of human beings is that of heaven and hell. This concept implies life of some kind beyond this present one with heaven being a reward for the good and hell being a punishment for the bad, but good and bad are highly subjective and relative concepts.

Are heaven and hell literal places? Is heaven in the sky and hell underground as we have been taught? Could it be that these places are purely metaphorical, symbolic, or states of mind? When we are in a state of bliss, we say we are in heaven. When we are distressed, we say we're in hell.

The literal notion of heaven being in the sky and hell being underground is a misnomer. Earth is hurling through space, which is in itself the heavens. It may be more suitable to say heaven is out there wherever we are. The idea of hell being underground may have been conceived at a time when the earth was identified as being flat; hence, heaven was any place above the earth with hell being any place below. Knowing however that the earth is spherical, ideologies of the existence of life in earth also known as the hollow-earth theory as proposed by Medal of Honor recipient Admiral Richard E. Byrd come to the fore. Was Admiral Byrd right about a world within our world with a central sun, cities, and advanced races? If so, could hell be an actual physical place in the earth?

According to the online etymology dictionary, heaven was derived from Old English *heofon*, the home of God and the visible sky. In the Old Testament, four Hebrew words are translated as heaven: *Rakia* means firmament; *Shamayim* can be identified in Genesis 1:1: "In the beginning God created the heaven and the earth"; *Maron* can be found in scriptures such as Psalm 18:16: "He sent from above, he took me, he drew me out of many waters"; the King James Version has "from above" while other versions have "from heaven" or "on high." A similar meaning is in Jeremiah 25:30 and Isaiah 24:18. Then there is the fourth—*Shechakim*, expanses as in Deuteronomy 33:26: "There is none like unto the God of Jeshurun, who rideth upon the heaven in thy help, and in his excellency on the sky." Job 35:5 and 2 Corinthians 12:2 are among other scriptures in which this meaning can be found. Of these four words, *Shamayim* is identified as the most common, and it is always plural.

In the New Testament, the Greek word *ouranos* is used for heaven, which correlates with the planet Uranus. Like many planets and other cosmological bodies however, the planet Uranus was personified, attributed humanistic characteristics. In ancient Greece, Uranus was identified as a god and was known as Father Sky, the son and husband of Gaia or Earth. From this one can recognize where the ideology of Mother Earth was derived.

The notion of personification can be identified in various texts and cultures including the Egyptian and Sumerian. In Egyptian mythology are the god Geb and the goddess Nut. Nut was the sister and wife of Geb, while Osiris, Isis, Seth, and Nephthys were their children. Geb represented the earth while Nut the sky; thus from the ancient Egyptian perspective, earth was masculine and identified as father earth as opposed to Greek mythology.

Personification is well noted in the Bible and Koran and Hindu scripts in which planets were given humanistic characteristics. Even the character identified as the devil or Lucifer was recognized as the morning star in Isaiah 14:12: "How you have fallen from heaven, O star of the morning, son of the dawn." In Malachi 4:2, we read, "But to you who fear My name The Sun of Righteousness shall arise With healing in His wings; And you shall go out And grow fat like stall-fed calves." Many claim that the sun referred to here describes the Son, but could it truly be that the Son was really the Sun personified? Contemporary ideologies such as astrotheology and the works of D. M. Murdock, Malik Jabbar, Bart D. Ehrman, and Santos Bonacci reveal much more on this concept.

So heaven is possibly more allegorical than literal. The notion of heaven's plurality however should be noted since it is identified that there exists several heavens; 2 Corinthians 12:2–3 reads, "I know a man in Christ who fourteen years ago—whether in the body I do not know, or whether out of the body I do not know, God knows—such a one was caught up to the third heaven." This scripture ascertains that there is more than one heaven, which can be observed. The first heaven refers to earth's atmosphere, which extends some twenty miles up; this is our immediate sky. Then there is the second heaven, what is termed the celestial heaven, which contains celestial bodies such as the sun, moon, and stars. And finally, there is the third heaven or what is called the heaven of heavens, which many refer to as the home of God.

Many authorities on the subject suggest that there exists more than three heavens. What many fail to understand though is the multidimensional nature of our universe. Besides the three heavens, which are spatially defined in a three-dimensional perspective, the heavens are also synonymous with the spiritual world, a world that is multidimensional in nature and beyond our three-dimensional reality. This understanding erodes the ideology of God being physically far away beyond the clouds and stars since the physical and spiritual realms exist parallel to each other. These realms interact and overlie the physical yet are unseen to the physical eye. The primary difference between the physical and spiritual realms has to do with vibratory states. It is these unseen realms that vibrate at much higher speeds that are identified as the causal realms.

In the same manner that our world is multidimensional in nature, so are we; yes, we are multidimensional beings. You may have heard the saying that we are spiritual beings having a physical experience; as such, we can vibrate at higher or lower frequencies. We can have such experiences while in a physical state, but upon our transition or death, when this physical state is discarded, we can proceed to exist in this heaven or hell, which are places that reflect our vibratory states.

The Hell Concept

In the Old Testament, *Sheol* was the only word for hell. In the New Testament, *Gehenna*, *Hades*, and *Tartarus* all meant hell. The Greek word Hades replaced Sheol from the Old Testament; thus, Hades and Sheol are purported to be synonymous. This however does not make its meaning any simpler, and I could not clarify that in my research. It would appear that in many instances where the words were used, their meaning was heavily dependent on the context in which it was used.

For instance, Hades, Sheol, or hell as we have been taught was a place for the souls of sinners or evildoers. It should be noted though that both the righteous and the unrighteous, believers and unbelievers went to this hell in the Old Testament. The distinction between the two was introduced in the New Testament, where hell was relegated to sinners, unbelievers and the unrighteous and where it became synonymous with fire and torture.

In many instances, Sheol or Hades is interpreted to mean a grave. This interpretation is questionable since *Qever* is the Hebrew word for grave. Hence, it is uncertain whether what was implied was a literal grave or an unseen realm where all must go. This concept of an abode or place known as the underworld however can be identified in various cultures historically.

Hades was the name of the Greek god of the underworld. He was the son of Cronus and Rhea and had five siblings—Zeus, Poseidon, Hestia, Demeter, and Hera. The story was that Hades kidnapped his niece Persephone, who was the daughter of his sister Demeter, and took her with him to the underworld.

This underworld in Egyptian mythology was known as *Duat*. Osiris, the god of death and reincarnation, was the god of Duat. Osiris was the eldest son of Geb and Nut, god of the earth and goddess of the sky respectively. He was the brother of Isis, Set, and Nephthys. Isis was also his wife through whom he fathered Horus. His other sister, Nephthys, also bore him a son, Anubis. The ideology of the underworld is in itself a journey for the soul of the departed through which the soul undergoes various steps that lead to a stage of being judged. This Egyptian saga was the first documented story of souls being judged in relation to their earthly deeds.

Various cultures share similar narratives about the underworld including the Sumerians, who called it the Land of No Return, which the goddess Ereshkigal ruled. Narratives pertaining to Ereshkigal such as "The Descent of Inanna" or "The Marriage of Ereshkigal and Nergal" bear striking similarities to the Egyptian myths of Osiris and Isis, the Greek myth of Demeter and Persephone, and that of Jesus Christ. In all instances, a god dies and is revived.

Another word used for hell in the New Testament is *Gehenna*, the Greek form of the Hebrew *Ge-hinnom*, the Valley of Hinnom. This was an actual location in Jerusalem where it was claimed that historically, children were sacrificed to gods such as Molech as is stipulated in Jeremiah 7:31: "And they have built the high places of Tophet, which is in the valley of the son of Hinnom, to burn their sons and their daughters in the fire; which I commanded them not, neither came it into my heart." Over time, this valley was transformed into a dumping ground where fire burned continuously fed by the city's sewage. In Mark 9:43, Jesus described hell, the afterlife, as Gehanna: "And if thy hand offend thee, cut it off: it is better for thee to enter into life maimed, than having two hands to go into hell, into the fire that never shall be quenched."

What type of fire did Jesus refer to though? The symbolism of fire is diverse, and its meaning can be highly dependent on the context in which it is used. Fire can be a destructive force, but it can also be a purifying force equated to birth and resurrection, regeneration, and divinity. Acts 2:3 describe tongues of fire coming to those in the Upper Room on the day of Pentecost.

The final word used for hell is Tartarus, used only once in the Bible, in 2 Peter 2:4: "God did not have pity on the angels that sinned. He had them tied up and thrown into the dark pits of hell until the time of judgment." Tartarus in Greek mythology in similar fashion to the word Hades describes both a place and a god. According to the Greek poet Hesiod in his epic the *Theogony*, which relates the myths of the gods, Tartarus was the third god to come alive at the beginning of time after Chaos and Gaea. It was also written that Tartarus and Gaea bore Typhon or Typhaon, a monster with numerous heads who was captured and cast in the underworld by Zeus. Again, the concept of an underworld was identified with Tartarus being even below Hades and a prison of sorts.

In Christianity, those who fail to accept Jesus as their Savior go to hell regardless of whether they were evil or good. Good and evil are highly subjective concepts, but we can all share stories about purported Christians who displayed much worse behavior than non-Christians. Christianity also implies that the most extreme sinners can escape hell even on their deathbeds by repenting and accepting Christ. This thought suggests that it's very possible that persons such as Hitler, Jeffrey Dahmer, and Ted Bundy could make it to heaven in spite of their hideous crimes.

Additionally, won't the notion of grace apply as it pertains to hell? And if so, to whom would this grace be given? Why can't God influence or convert hearts as he did when he hardened Pharaoh's heart in Exodus 9:12: "And the LORD hardened the heart of Pharaoh, and he hearkened not unto them; as the LORD had spoken unto Moses"? The concept we have been taught about hell is not one perpetuated in either Eastern or Jewish philosophies. Hell cannot be a place where people go as a result of retributive punishment since we are not judged for our sins but by our sins themselves.

Based on my research, it appears that the intention of the hell and heaven concepts perpetuated over generations had one objective—to threaten those who sinned and reward those who were good. This fear-based doctrine contradicted scripture from which it sprung; 2 Timothy 1:7 tells us, "God is not the author of fear." No fear-based strategy could be on God's agenda. This observation does not nullify the existence of hell, but it certainly seeks to address the concept.

As is heaven, hell is multidimensional and vibratory. The experiences that people may have are determined only by themselves as their beliefs, emotions, and states of consciousness act as determinants in their reality both within and beyond this three-dimensional experience. In my mind, hell is simply a refining fire designed to help eradicate conditioned elements attached to the soul for its purification. It would appear that the basis of our existence in this form has to do with the evolution of our souls and that this process continues even beyond our physical existence. It appears that this three-dimensional state on earth is a sort of middle ground where based on the decisions we make, we go to the higher, the realm of heaven, or to the lower, the realm of hell.

The notion of the underworld in Egyptian culture suggests different phases of purification the soul must go through with the final stage being called Maat, justice. Placing one's heart on a scale and it being balanced with a feather symbolically represents this final stage. It reasons that justice is not based on any punitive measures but is a refining process where one fully repents and converts from being dense and dark to light and subsequently proceeding beyond.

CONCLUSION

Our beliefs and values shape our attitudes and determine our behaviors. This means that if we can address our core beliefs, that could ultimately lead to a change in our behavior. If our behavior can be altered not as a result of legislation or other external factors but from a position of greater understanding of the meaning life, of what we truly are, our comportment would follow.

In *Culture Matters*, Professor Lawrence Harrison expounded on the various forms of capital of which cultural capital was determined to be the most significant. Cultural capital is based on the core values and beliefs of a population including its religious beliefs, which can operate subliminally. Cultural capital determines whether a nation was developed or in a state of perpetual development; this was the determining factor in what separates First World from Third World nations.

With this information, one would get a clearer understanding why what we believe is so important, especially our religious beliefs. Historically and contemporarily, religious beliefs are at the center of most of our conflicts and wars. What most of us have failed to recognize though is that they are only beliefs. A belief is not necessarily a fact, and what we believe and hold onto as guiding principles are not necessarily based on substance but on perceptions and conjecture.

Our lives are too significant to be guided by dogmas and ideologies that do not serve the collective or ourselves. If the concepts we have been conditioned to accept are false, gaining any further understanding would be restricted by these concepts since they are our proverbial boxes. We can start thinking outside our boxes only when we question those boxes. Can a box contain what we are now beginning to understand?

The Socratic paradox derived from Plato's account of the Greek philosopher Socrates states, "The only thing I know is that I know nothing." This quote at best identifies my cognitive state prior to and after my research for this book. What do we truly know? All we supposedly know about anything is perceptions of reality and fractions of the truth, and as much as we research and discover, the more we unearth, the less we recognize that we actually know. Many times, I placed my head in the sand and sought to dismiss whatever I could not assimilate and whatever was not supported by those acclaimed to be authorities in the field. Many times, I felt ridiculed, embarrassed, and fearful for asking, speaking, and possibly accepting the ideas and concepts I did. Was it unfair to consider that an all-knowing God would have known the conclusion to all of this we call life and thus make it redundant? It's possible though that the concept we have of this God is wrong.

How could one possibly ignore clear historical disparities in time between what the religious identify as opposed to evidence scientists and archeologists present? How can one disregard the existence of cultures and civilizations such as Egypt and Sumer, whose history predates what religious ideology purports, and the distinct similarities between characters of both eras? What about that gut feeling one gets as it pertains to extraterrestrial life and the personal experience of so many? Should one ignore such core feelings and discount all the reports and personal experiences of those who may have had near-death experiences as lies and simply a motive for attracting attention?

We have seen the diverse perspectives that exist as they pertain to religious dogmas; how should we select which one to follow? What if none resonates with what we feel? Knowing that the meaning of anything is determined only by interpretation influenced by context and consciousness, what really can we identify as *the* truth? Does such an ideal exist?

Every day, new discoveries are being made in science and other fields that advance knowledge. Life continues to evolve; change is the only constant.

Where have the gods of the Aztecs and Incas gone? Where have the gods of the Greeks and the Egyptians gone? Is it possible that in a few generations, people will be asking the same question about our God or gods? Does the ideology of God exist only because humanity exists and as humanity evolves so does God? With the advent of the quantum world and the understanding of the power of thought and consciousness, we recognize that we are not merely in the universe but part and parcel of it, active participants whether we accept that or not. How would such understanding influence our near future?

We can't deny a conscious awakening of sorts that appears to be happening globally. A shift is taking place on all spheres—mentally, emotionally, spiritually, and otherwise. Questions are being asked that were never asked before, and the answers are forthcoming. History and our present societal state would validate that what we may have been doing or believing may not have been serving us very well. Laws intimidate and direct by fear while understanding allows one to act from a place of love.

I wrote this book to help others reconsider what they think they know or believe. I hope that my readers will open themselves to the new, to different paradigms, and become more of whom they were designed to be.

REFERENCES

Bauer, Walter. *Orthodoxy and Heresy in Earliest Christianity.* Dallas: Sigler Press, 1996.

Ehrman, D. Bart. *Misquoting Jesus: The Story Behind Who Changed the Bible and Why.* San Francisco: Harper One, 2005.

Ehrman, D. Bart. *Jesus Interrupted.* San Francisco: Harper One, 2009.

Furneaux, Rupert. *The Other Side of the Story.* London: Cassell and Co., 1953.

Doane, T. W. *Bible Myths and Their Parallels in Other Religions.* New York: Forgotten Books, Cosimo Classics, 2012.

Rops, H. Daniel. *The Church in the Dark Ages.* Vol. 1. Garden City: Image Books, 1962

Stone, Merlin. *When God Was a Woman.* London: Marboro Books, 1990.

Myss, Caroline. *Archetypes.* Hay House, CA, January 8, 2013.

Gage, Joslyn Matilda. *Woman, Church and State.* London: Persephone Press, 1980.

Jackson, G. John. *Christianity Before Christ.* Texas: American Atheist Press, 1985.

Jackson, G. John. *Man, God and Civilization.* Bensenville, IL: Lushena Books, 2000.

Churchward, Albert. *The Origin and Evolution of Religion.* Bensenville, IL: Lushena Books, 2003.

Friedman, Elliot Richard. *Who Wrote the Bible?* San Francisco: Harper One, 1997.

Mead, G. R. S. *Pistis Sophia: A Gnostic Bible*. London: University Books, 2012.

Wright, Robert. *The Evolution of God*. Boston: Little Brown & Company, 2009.

Shelby, Alex. The *Evolution of Religion*. Scotts Valley, CA: Createspace Independent Publishing Platform, 2014.

Jabbar, H. Malik. *The Biggest Lie Ever Told*. Ohio: Rare Books, 2006.

CPSIA information can be obtained
at www.ICGtesting.com
Printed in the USA
BVHW081351090620
580983BV00001B/5